# Important Instruction

Students, Parents, and Teachers can use the URL or QR code provided below to access two full-length Lumos OST practice tests. Please note that these assessments are provided in the Online format only.

| URL | QR Code |
|---|---|
| Visit the URL below and place the book access code<br><br>**http://www.lumoslearning.com/a/tedbooks**<br><br>**Access Code: OSTG6E-30179-P** |  |

**Lumos Learning**
Developed by Expert Teachers

# Ohio State Test Prep: Grade 6 English Language Arts Literacy (ELA) Practice Workbook and Full-length Online Assessments: OST Study Guide

| | | |
|---|---|---|
| **Contributing Editor** | - | **Heather Dorey** |
| **Contributing Editor** | - | **Janet Redell** |
| **Contributing Editor** | - | **George Smith** |
| **Executive Producer** | - | **Mukunda Krishnaswamy** |
| **Designer and Illustrator** | - | **Harini N.** |

## First Edition - 2020

ISBN-10: 1-945730-45-5

ISBN-13: 978-1-945730-45-0

Printed in the United States of America

### For permissions and additional information contact us

Lumos Information Services, LLC
PO Box 1575, Piscataway, NJ 08855-1575
http://www.LumosLearning.com

Email: support@lumoslearning.com
Tel: (732) 384-0146
Fax: (866) 283-6471

Developed by Expert Teachers

# INTRODUCTION

This book is specifically designed to improve student achievement on the Ohio State Test (OST). With over a decade of expertise in developing practice resources for standardized tests, Lumos Learning has designed the most efficient methodology to help students succeed on the state assessments (See Figure 1).

Lumos Smart Test Prep Methodology provides students OST assessment rehearsal along with an efficient pathway to overcome any standards proficiency gaps. Students perform at their best on standardized tests when they feel comfortable with the test content as well as the test format. Lumos online practice tests are meticulously designed to mirror the OST assessment. It adheres to the guidelines provided by the OST for the number of questions, standards, difficulty level, sessions, question types, and duration.

The process starts with students taking the online diagnostic assessment. This online diagnostic test will help assess students' proficiency levels in various standards.

After completion of the diagnostic assessment, students can take note of standards where they are not proficient. This step will help parents and educators in developing a targeted remedial study plan based on a student's proficiency gaps.

Once the targeted remedial study plan is in place, students can start practicing the lessons in this workbook that are focused on specific standards.

After the student completes the targeted remedial practice, the student should attempt the second online OST practice test. Record the proficiency levels in the second practice test to measure the student progress and identify any additional learning gaps. Further targeted practice can be planned to help students gain comprehensive skills mastery needed to ensure success on the state assessment.

## Lumos Smart Test Prep Methodology

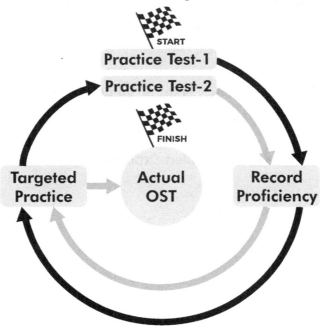

Figure 1

# Table of Contents

# Sign Up Online

# OST

## Grade 6 ELA Practice

**Unlock Digital Access**

**2** OST Practice Tests

**3** ELA Strands

**Sign Up Now**

Url: https://LumosLearning/a/tedbooks

Access Code: OSTG6E-30179-P

# Access OST Test Practice Resources On Your Mobile Device

| Online Access | | Printed Workbook |
|:---:|:---:|:---:|
| for | | for |
| OST Practice | **+** | Skills Practice |

## Download Lumos StepUp App
### from Google Play Store or Apple App Store

After installing the StepUp App, scan this **QR Code** via **tedBook** section of the mobile app

# Chapter 1
# Lumos Smart Test Prep Methodology

## Step 1: Access Online OST Practice Test

The online OST practice tests mirror the actual Ohio State Test(OST) in the number of questions, item types, test duration, test tools, and more.

After completing the test, your student will receive immediate feedback with detailed reports on standards mastery and a personalized study plan to overcome any learning gaps. With this study plan, use the next section of the workbook to practice.

**Use the URL and access code provided below or scan the QR code to access the first OST practice test to get started.**

| URL | QR Code |
|---|---|
| Visit the URL below and place the book access code<br><br>**http://www.lumoslearning.com/a/tedbooks**<br><br>**Access Code: OSTG6E-30179-P** |  |

# Step 2: Review the Personalized Study Plan Online

After students complete the online Practice Test 1, they can access their individualized study plan from the table of contents (Figure 2) Parents and Teachers can also review the study plan through their Lumos account (parent or teacher) portal.

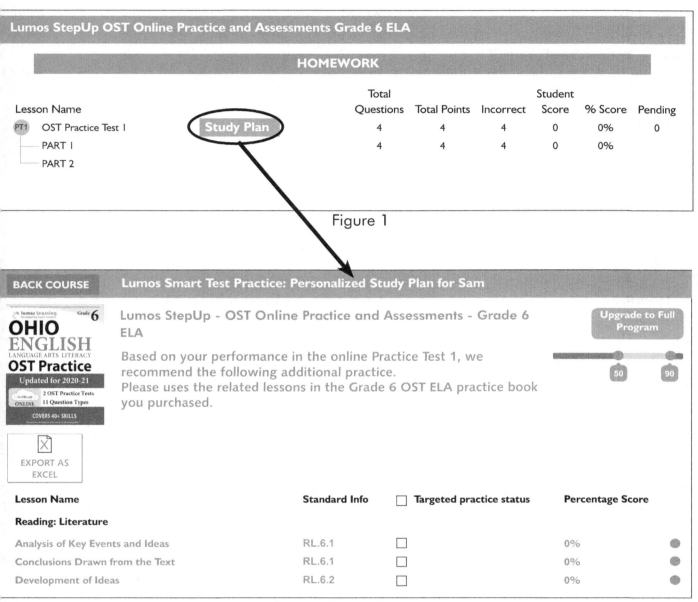

Figure 1

Figure 2

# Step 3: Complete Targeted Practice

Using the information provided in the study plan report, complete the targeted practice using the appropriate lessons to overcome proficiency gaps. With lesson names included in the study plan find the appropriate topics in this workbook and answer the questions provided. Students can refer to the answer key and detailed answers provided for each lesson to gain further understanding of the learning objective. Marking the completed lessons in the study plan after each practice session is recommended.(See Figure 3)

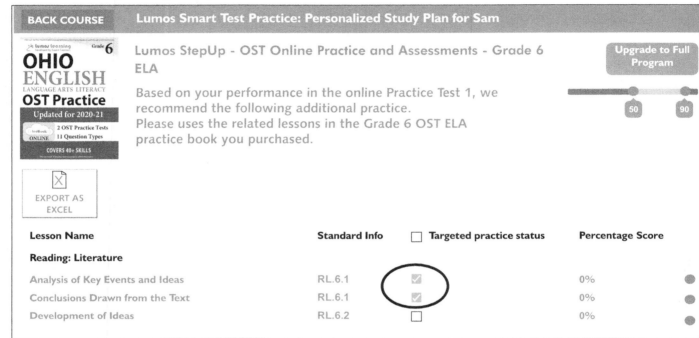

Figure 3

# Step 4: Access the Practice Test 2 Online

After completing the targeted practice in this workbook, students should attempt the second OST practice test online. Using the student login name and password, login to the Lumos website to complete the second practice test.

# Step 5: Repeat Targeted Practice

Repeat the targeted practice as per Step 3 using the second study plan report for Practice test 2 after completion of the second OST rehearsal.

Visit http://www.lumoslearning.com/a/lstp for more information on Lumos Smart Test Prep Methodology or Scan the QR Code

# Test Taking Tips

1) **The day before the test,** make sure you get a good night's sleep.

2) **On the day of the test,** be sure to eat a good hearty breakfast! Also, be sure to arrive at school on time.

3) **During the test:**

- **Read every question carefully.**

  - Do not spend too much time on any one question. Work steadily through all questions in the section.
  - Attempt all of the questions even if you are not sure of some answers.
  - If you run into a difficult question, eliminate as many choices as you can and then pick the best one from the remaining choices. Intelligent guessing will help you increase your score.
  - Also, mark the question so that if you have extra time, you can return to it after you reach the end of the section.
  - Some questions may refer to a graph, chart, or other kind of picture. Carefully review the infographics before answering the question.
  - Be sure to include explanations for your written responses and show all work.

- **While Answering EBSR questions.**

  - EBSR questions come in 2 parts - PART A and B.
  - Both PART A and B could be multiple choice or Part A could be multiple choice while Part B could be some other type.
  - Generally, Part A and B will be related, sometimes it may just be from the same lesson but not related questions.
  - If it is a Multiple choice question, Select the bubble corresponding to your answer choice.
  - Read all of the answer choices, even if think you have found the correct answer.
  - In case the questions in EBSR are not multiple choice questions, follow the instruction for other question types while answering such questions.

- **While Answering TECR questions.**

  - Read the directions of each question. Some might ask you to drag something, others to select, and still others to highlight. Follow all instructions of the question (or questions if it is in multiple parts)

# Chapter 2 - Reading: Literature

The objective of the Reading Literature standards is to ensure that the student is able to read and comprehend literature (which includes stories, dramas and poetry) related to Grade 6.

To help students master the necessary skills, information to help the student understand the concepts related to the standard is given. Along with this, we encourage the student to go through the resources available online on EdSearch to gain an in depth understanding of these concepts. The EdSearch page for each lesson can be accessed with the help of the URL or the QR code provided.

A small map is provided after each passage or text in which the student can enter the details as understood from the literary text. Doing this will help the student refer to key points that help in answering the questions with ease.

# Chapter 2

## Lesson 1: Analysis of Key Events and Ideas

**Definitions:**

1. Cite (textual evidence) means the same as name or quote or mention (textual evidence).

2. Explicitly means clearly expressed.

3. Inferences means conclusions reached or judgments made after reading and thinking about the meaning of a statement or proposal. These conclusions or judgments are not included in the statement or proposal.

*Let us understand the concept with an example.*

### The Obesity Epidemic

In the United States population, 30% of adults and 17% of children are obese according to the American Heart Association. And by 2020, 83% of men and 72% of women are expected to be overweight or obese, according to research presented to the Heart Association's scientific meeting in 2011. More than one-third (36.5%) of U.S. adults have obesity, states the Centers for Disease Control and Prevention.

Being obese has negative health and health expense disadvantages. According to the Centers for Disease Control and Prevention:

- Obesity-related conditions include heart disease, stroke, type 2 diabetes, high blood pressure, arthritis and certain types of cancer - some of the leading causes of preventable death.

- The estimated annual medical cost of obesity in the U.S. was $147 billion U.S. dollars in 2008; the medical costs for people who are obese were $1,429 higher than those of normal weight.

What is causing so many people to be obese? More sedentary lifestyles are one factor. Sitting and watching television, driving instead of walking, not exercising enough. Nutrition is another. So much of our food is processed, which means fat and sugar are added. Also, we frequently eat portions larger than our bodies need, and we often snack between meals.

**What can people do about reducing their obesity?**

- Exercise: The Centers for Disease Control (CDC) recommends 2.5 hours of moderate aerobic exercise per week, along with 2 days of strength training. Americans are clearly not abiding by these minimum recommendations. But diet can have more effect on weight loss than exercise, althoug both are important solutions.

- Nutrition: Controlling the intake of carbohydrates is one important action. Also, eating less pro cessed food, less refined grains and bread and more vegetables are also important. You need t add lean protein to every meal and every snack, along with moderate amounts of healthy fats.

- An article in a fitness newsletter, published by a leading chain of physical fitness centers, empha sizes that participating daily in their fitness plans will result in losing weight, building enduranc and increasing muscle tone.

Your assignment: Write text that meets the requirements of the standard.

**Here is what you might write.**

The authors state that there is an obesity epidemic today among adults and children in America. The cite statistics from the American Heart Association and the Centers for Disease Control and Preven tion as proof. Because these two organizations are reputable and trustworthy, I believe that their argu ments are relevant and accurate.

The authors also state that being obese has negative health and health expense disadvantages, an list diseases associated with obesity and the medical costs incurred by obese people. These facts wer also provided by the Centers for Disease Control and Prevention. I checked with two family doctor and both agreed with the list of diseases. Therefore, I support these facts as accurate. The author also speculate on the causes of the obesity epidemic, citing a more sedentary lifestyle, insufficien exercise and dietary factors. I have observed many fellow students, and the lifestyles of most of them fit these three causes of obesity. My parents also subscribe to a newsletter edited by a nutritionist, an it cites the same conclusions about the causes of obesity.

Lastly, the authors state what can be done to reduce obesity, citing suggestions for exercise and nu trition. These suggestions are also in line with the newsletter and with the recommendations of tw trainers at my parent's physical fitness center.

However, the recommendations from an article in a newsletter published by a for-profit fitness cente are not specific in providing data to support its claims about the benefits of participating in its pro grams, inferring that maybe the claims are not true.

Name: _____     Date: _____

You can scan the QR code given below or use the URL to access additional EdSearch resources including videos and mobile apps related to *Analysis of Key Events and Ideas.*

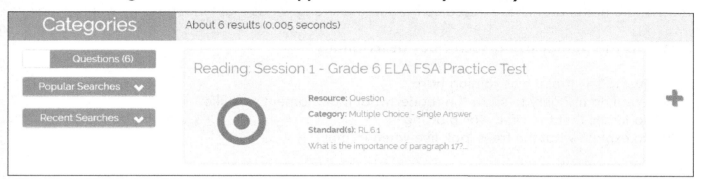

**Categories**

About 6 results (0.005 seconds)

Questions (6)

Popular Searches ∨

Recent Searches ∨

Reading: Session 1 - Grade 6 ELA FSA Practice Test

**Resource:** Question

**Category:** Multiple Choice - Single Answer

**Standard(s):** RL.6.1

What is the importance of paragraph 17?...

+

 **ed)Search**

## *Analysis of Key Events and Ideas*

| URL | QR Code |
|---|---|
| http://www.lumoslearning.com/a/rl61 | |

As it poured outside, I settled down by the window to watch the rain. The green park opposite my house looked even more green and fresh than usual. Strong winds shook the branches of the tall trees. Some of the branches swayed so hard in the strong winds that I thought they would break.

**1. Why is the author using such clear descriptions?**

    Ⓐ  just to say that it was raining hard
    Ⓑ  creating imagery to show the reader what that moment was like
    Ⓒ  to tell us that the wind was blowing
    Ⓓ  to explain what the trees look like when it rains

# The Forest's Sentinel

At night, when all is still
The forest's sentinel
Glides silently across the hill
And perches in an old pine tree,
A friendly presence his!
No harm can come
From night bird on the prowl.
His cry is mellow,
Much softer than a peacock's call.
Why then this fear of owls
Calling in the night?
If men must speak,
Then owls must hoot-
They have the right.
On me it casts no spell:
Rather, it seems to cry,
"The night is good- all's well, all's well."
-- RUSKIN BOND

**2. From what point of view is the above poem?**

    Ⓐ  First person point of view - from the owl's perspective
    Ⓑ  3rd person point of view - from an unknown bystander or the author
    Ⓒ  First person point of view - from another animal's perspective
    Ⓓ  None of the above

3. According to the above poem when does the Owl come out?

Ⓐ   at night
Ⓑ   at dawn
Ⓒ   at dusk
Ⓓ   at noon

Once upon a time, four boys lived in the countryside. One boy was very clever, but he did not like books. His name was Good Sense. The other boys were not very clever, but they read every book in the school. When they became grown men, they decided to go out into the world to earn their livelihood.

They left home and came to a forest where they halted for the night. When they woke up in the morning, they found the bones of a lion. Three of them, who had learned their books well at school, decided to make a lion out of the bones.

Good Sense told them, "A lion is a dangerous animal. It will kill us. Don't make a lion." But the three disregarded his advice and started making a lion. Good Sense was very clever. When his friends were busy making the lion, he climbed up a tree to save himself. No sooner had the three young men created the lion and gave it life, than it pounced upon them and ate them up. Good Sense climbed down the tree and went home very sadly.

**After reading the story, enter the details in the map below. This will help you answer the questions with ease.**

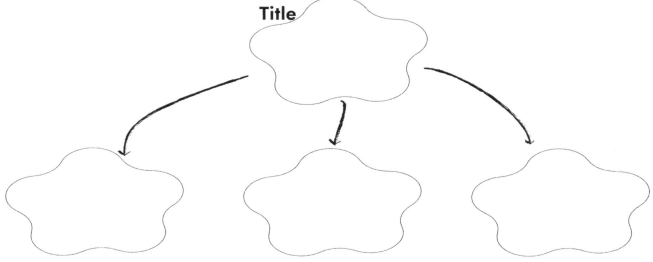

Characters                Supporting Details                Main Idea

**4. Part A**
**What did they see in the forest when they woke up in the morning?**

Ⓐ  the bones of a lion
Ⓑ  a witch that could bring an animal to life
Ⓒ  Good Sense hiding in a tree
Ⓓ  none of the above

**Part B**
**What did the four friends decide when they became grown men?**

Ⓐ  They decided to go out into the world and earn their livelihood.
Ⓑ  They decided to play with animal bones.
Ⓒ  They decided to be friends forever.
Ⓓ  They decided to never leave home.

**5. What advice did Good Sense give his friends?**

Ⓐ  He told them how to create the lion.
Ⓑ  He told them how to beat the lion once it was created.
Ⓒ  He told them not to create the lion.
Ⓓ  He told them to hide from the lion once they created it.


One evening, long after most people had gone to bed, a friend and I were making our way merril
back home through the silent and almost deserted streets. We had been to a musical show and wer
talking about the actor we had seen and heard in it.

"That show made him a star overnight," said my friend about one of the actors. "He was completel
unknown before, and now thousands of teenagers send him chocolates and love letters through th
mail."

"I thought he was quite good," I said, "but not worth thousands of love letters daily. As a matter o
fact, one of his songs gave me pain."

"What was that?" my friend asked. "Sing to me." I burst into a parody of the song.

"Be quiet for heaven's sake!" My friend gave me an astonished look. "You'll give everybody a frigh
and wake people for miles around."

"Never mind," I said, intoxicated with the sound of my own voice. "I don't care. Why does it matter?

And I went on singing the latest tunes at the top of my voice.

Suddenly, there came behind us the sound of heavy footsteps, and before you could say "Jack Robinson," a policeman was standing in front of me, his notebook open, and a determined look on his face.

"Excuse me, sir," he said. "You have a remarkable voice if I may say so. Who taught you to sing? I'd very much like to find someone who can give my daughter singing lessons. Would you be kind enough to tell me your name and address? Then my wife or I can drop you a line and discuss the matter."

**After reading the story, enter the details in the map below. This will help you answer the question with ease.**

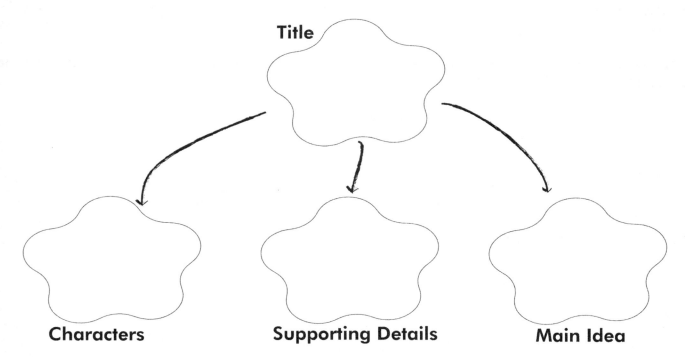

**6. Why was the friend telling the man singing to be quiet?**

Ⓐ   He did not like the sound of the singer's voice.
Ⓑ   He was embarrassed.
Ⓒ   He was worried that it would wake people for miles around.
Ⓓ   Because the policeman told them to be quiet.

The sky was dark and overcast. It had been raining all night long, and there was no sign of it stopping. I thought that my Sunday would be ruined. As it poured outside, I settled down by the window to watch the rain. The park opposite my house looked even more green and fresh than usual. The branches of the tall trees swayed so hard in the strong wind that I thought they would break. A few children were splashing about in the mud puddles and having a wonderful time. I wished I could join them too! There were very few people out on the road and those who were hurried on their way, wrapped in raincoats and carrying umbrellas.

My mother announced that lunch was ready. It was piping hot and very welcoming in the damp weather. We spent the afternoon listening to music and to the downpour outside.

In the evening, we chatted and made paper boats that we meant to sail in the stream of water outside. It was not a bad day, after all!

**After reading the story, enter the details in the map below. This will help you answer the question with ease.**

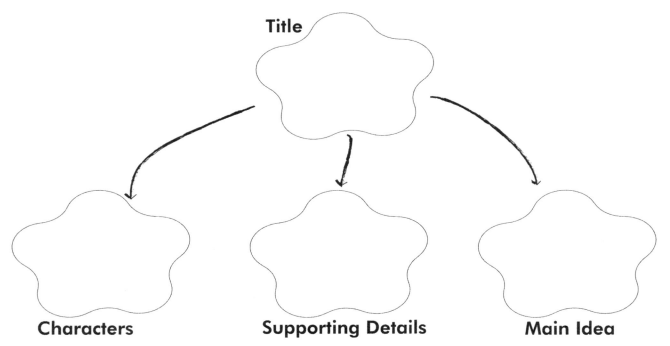

**Title**

**Characters**          **Supporting Details**          **Main Idea**

**7. What detail in the above passage tells us that the writer yearned to play outside?**

Ⓐ  The park opposite my house looked even more green and fresh.
Ⓑ  We spent the afternoon listening to music and to the downpour outside.
Ⓒ  I wished I could join them too!
Ⓓ  All of the above

Faster than fairies, faster than witches,
Bridges and houses, hedges and ditches,
And charging along like troops in a battle,
All through the meadows the horses and cattle,
All of the sights of the hill and the plain,
Fly as thick as driving rain,
And ever again, in the wink of an eye,
Painted stations whistle by.

Here is a child who clambers and scrambles,
All by himself and gathering brambles;
Here is a tramp who stands and gazes,
And there is the green for stinging the daisies;
Here is a cart run away in the road,
Jumping along with man and load;
And here is a mill and there is a river,
Each a glimpse and gone forever.
- R. L. STEVENSON

**3. What detail in the above poem tells us that this poem is about the view from inside a train?**

    Ⓐ   All of the sights of the hill and the plain, Fly as thick as driving rain
    Ⓑ   Faster than fairies, faster than witches, Bridges and houses, hedges and ditches,
    Ⓒ   And ever again, in the wink of an eye, Painted stations whistle by.
    Ⓓ   Here is a cart run away in the road

# Excerpt from Arabian Nights, Aladdin

After these words, the magician drew a ring off his finger, and put it on one of Aladdin's, telling him that it was a preservative against all evil, while he should observe what he had prescribed to him. After this instruction he said: "Go down boldly, child, and we shall both be rich all our lives."

Aladdin jumped into the cave, descended the steps, and found the three halls just as the African magician had described. He went through them with all the precaution the fear of death could inspire; crossed the garden without stopping, took down the lamp from the niche, threw out the wick and the liquor, and, as the magician had desired, put it in his vestband. But as he came down from the terrace, he stopped in the garden to observe the fruit, which he only had a glimpse of in crossing it. All the trees were loaded with extraordinary fruit, of different colors on each tree. Some bore fruit entirely white, and some clear and transparent as crystal; some pale red, and others deeper; some green, blue, and purple, and others yellow: in short, there were fruits of all colors. The white were pearls; the clear and transparent, diamonds; the deep red, rubies; the green, emeralds; the blue, turquoises; the purple, amethysts; and those that were of yellow cast, sapphires. Aladdin was altogether ignorant

of their worth, and would have preferred figs and grapes, or any other fruits. But though he too
them only for colored glass of little value, yet he was so pleased with the variety of the colors, an
the beauty and extraordinary size of the seeming fruit, that he resolved to gather some of every sor
and accordingly filled the two new purses his uncle had bought for him with his clothes. Some h
wrapped up in the skirts of his vest, which was of silk, large and full, and he crammed his bosom a
full as it could hold.

Aladdin, having thus loaded himself with riches, returned through the three halls with the same pre
caution, made all the haste he could, that he might not make his uncle wait, and soon arrived at th
mouth of the cave, where the African magician expected him with the utmost impatience. As soon a
Aladdin saw him, he cried out: "Pray, uncle, lend me your hand, to help me out." "Give me the lamp
first," replied the magician; "it will be troublesome to you." "Indeed, uncle," answered Aladdin, "
cannot now; it is not troublesome to me: but I will as soon as I am up." The African magician was s
obstinate, that he would have the lamp before he would help him up; and Aladdin, who had encum
bered himself so much with his fruit that he could not well get at it, refused to give it to him till he wa
out of the cave. The African magician, provoked at this obstinate refusal, flew into a passion, threw
little of his incense into the fire, which he had taken care to keep in, and no sooner pronounced tw
magical words, than the stone which had closed the mouth of the cave moved into its place, with th
earth over it in the same manner as it lay at the arrival of the magician and Aladdin.

**9. What did the magician put on one of Aladdin's fingers? Write your answer in the bo
below.**

```
╭─────────────────────────────────╮
│                                 │
│                                 │
│                                 │
╰─────────────────────────────────╯
```

# Chapter 2

## Lesson 2: Conclusions Drawn from the Text

You can scan the QR code given below or use the url to access additional EdSearch resources including videos and mobile apps related to *Conclusions Drawn from the Text*.

 Search

## Conclusions Drawn from the Text

| URL | QR Code |
| --- | --- |
| http://www.lumoslearning.com/a/rl61 |  |

Sarah's mother told her to carry an umbrella on that Thursday morning before she left home for school, but Sarah did not want to do that. She already had her backpack and a gift for her friend to take with her. She just did not think it was necessary.

**After reading the story, enter the details in the map below. This will help you answer the questions with ease.**

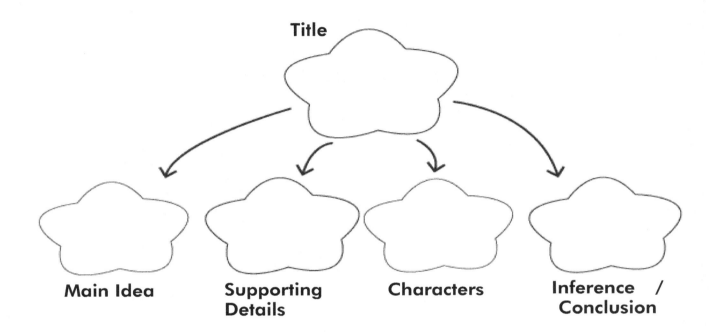

**1. What can you infer about Sarah?**

Ⓐ  She is stubborn and only wants to do things if they seem right to her.
Ⓑ  She does not like her mother.
Ⓒ  She doesn't like getting wet.
Ⓓ  She is a very obedient child.

**2. What can you infer about the weather on that Thursday morning?**

Ⓐ  It was raining.
Ⓑ  It was snowing.
Ⓒ  It was going to rain.
Ⓓ  It was a warm day.

The boy returned home a little late from school. He threw his coat as he walked in. He walked past his parents without greeting them. He headed straight to his room, slamming the door after him. He threw himself face down on his bed and lay there.

**After reading the story, enter the details in the map below. This will help you answer the question with ease.**

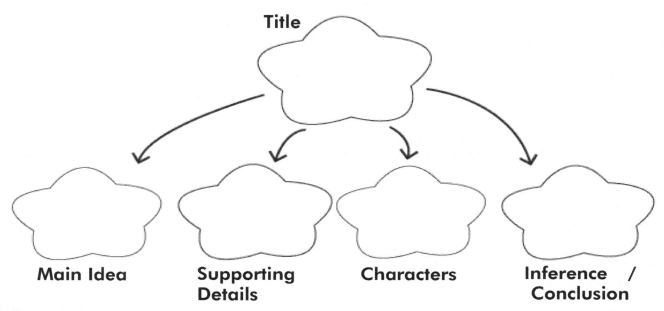

**3. How is he feeling?**

- Ⓐ  very delighted
- Ⓑ  very disappointed
- Ⓒ  very scared
- Ⓓ  very excited

Katie called out to her mother. The aroma of freshly brewed coffee filled the air. The sizzling sound of frying eggs reached her ears as she glided down the stairs. Now she could smell toast and bacon too. She ran to the table and sank into her seat just as her mother walked in from the kitchen. She was ready for _____

**4. Complete the sentence above.**

- Ⓐ  Dinner
- Ⓑ  Lunch
- Ⓒ  Breakfast
- Ⓓ  Sleeping

John wanted to buy some candy at the store. When he got there he realized he forgot his money.

**5. What can you infer as the action that John could take that would have the most chance of succeeding?**

Ⓐ   John asked the store owner if he could pay him back another day.
Ⓑ   John asked the store owner if he could work for the candy.
Ⓒ   John walked outside and looked on the ground to see if anyone dropped money.
Ⓓ   John walked back home and got the money he forgot.

Once upon a time, four boys lived in the countryside. One boy was very clever, but he did not lik books. His name was Good Sense. The other boys were not very clever, but they read every book i the school. When they became grown men, they decided to go out into the world to earn their liveli hood.

They left home and came to a forest where they halted for the night. When they woke up in the morn ing, they found the bones of a lion. Three of them, who had learnt their books well at school, decide to make a lion out of the bones.

Good Sense told them, "A lion is a dangerous animal. It will kill us. Don't make a lion." But the thre disregarded his advice and started making a lion. Good Sense was very clever. When his friend were busy making the lion, he climbed up a tree to save himself. No sooner had the three young me created the lion and gave it life, than it pounced upon them and ate them up. Good Sense climbe down the tree and went home very sadly.

**After reading the story, enter the details in the map below. This will help you answer th question with ease.**

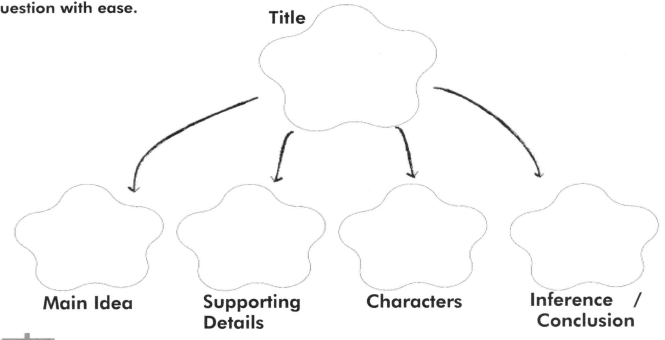

Title

Main Idea          Supporting Details          Characters          Inference / Conclusion

## 6. Which of the following statement(s) is true about Good Sense?

Ⓐ  He was very clever
Ⓑ  He did not like books
Ⓒ  He did not like the other boys
Ⓓ  Both A and B

It is recommended that people should exercise every day, particularly those who spend many hours doing sedentary activities like playing cards, reading, or playing video games.

## 7. We can infer that when people are doing sedentary activities, they must be _____.

Ⓐ  Running
Ⓑ  Talking
Ⓒ  Sitting
Ⓓ  Jumping

The sky was dark and overcast. It had been raining all night long, and there was no sign of it stopping. I thought that my Sunday would be ruined. As it poured outside, I settled down by the window to watch the rain. The park opposite my house looked even more green and fresh than usual. The branches of the tall trees swayed so hard in the strong wind that I thought they would break. A few children were splashing about in the mud puddles and having a wonderful time. I wished I could join them too! There were very few people out on the road and those who were hurried on their way, wrapped in raincoats and carrying umbrellas.

My mother announced that lunch was ready. It was piping hot and very welcoming in the damp weather. We spent the afternoon listening to music and to the downpour outside.

In the evening, we chatted and made paper boats that we meant to sail in the stream of water outside. It was not a bad day, after all!

After reading the story, enter the details in the map below. This will help you answer the question with ease.

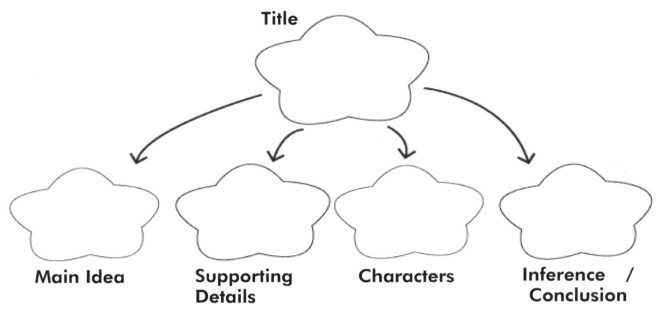

**Title**

**Main Idea**    **Supporting Details**    **Characters**    **Inference / Conclusion**

**8. When did the event described in the passage occur?**

- Ⓐ  On a very nice and sunny day.
- Ⓑ  On a wintry day.
- Ⓒ  On a hot day.
- Ⓓ  On a rainy day.

One evening, long after most people had gone to bed, a friend and I were making our way merrily back home through the silent and almost deserted streets. We had been to a musical show and were talking about the actor we had seen and heard in it.

"That show made him a star overnight," said my friend about one of the actors. "He was completely unknown before, and now thousands of teenagers send him chocolates and love letters through the mail."

"I thought he was quite good," I said, "but not worth thousands of love letters daily. As a matter of fact, one of his songs gave me pain."

"What was that?" my friend asked. "Sing to me." I burst into a parody of the song.

"Be quiet for heaven's sake!" My friend gave me an astonished look. "You'll give everybody a fright and wake people up for miles around."

"Never mind," I said, intoxicated with the sound of my own voice. "I don't care. How does it matter?"

And I went on singing the latest tunes at the top of my voice.

Presently there came behind us the sound of heavy footsteps, and before you could say "Jack Robinson," a policeman was standing in front of me, his notebook open, and a determined look on his face.

"Excuse me, sir," he said. "You have a remarkable voice if I may say so. Who taught you to sing? I'd very much like to find someone who can give my daughter singing lessons. Would you be kind enough to tell me your name and address? Then my wife or I can drop you a line and discuss the matter."

**After reading the story, enter the details in the map below. This will help you answer the question with ease.**

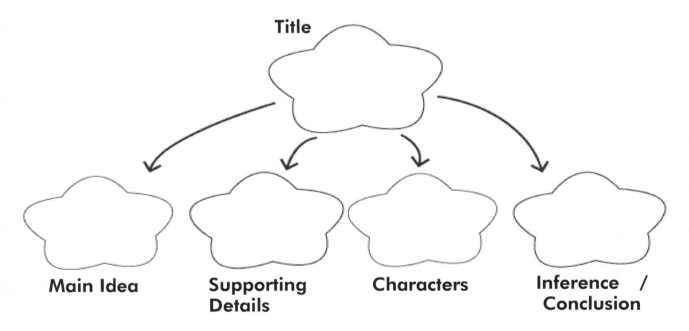

**Title**

**Main Idea**   **Supporting Details**   **Characters**   **Inference / Conclusion**

9. **Which detail in the above paragraph tells us that the author of the above passage is a male?**

Ⓐ   "He was completely unknown before"
Ⓑ   "And I went on singing the latest tunes at the top of my voice"
Ⓒ   "Excuse me, sir," he said
Ⓓ   "You have a remarkable voice"

The boy and his dog were watching television when they heard a loud bang. There was a thunder storm outside and the boy guessed that lightning must have hit something. The dog started to whim per and hid under the table.
You can guess that _____.

**10. Complete the sentence above.**

    Ⓐ  the dog was scared of the television show.
    Ⓑ  the dog was in trouble.
    Ⓒ  the dog was scared of the thunderstorm.
    Ⓓ  the dog needed to go outside.

The leaves were changing colors and there were pumpkins in people's yards.

**11. What season is it?**

The leaves were changing colors and there were pumpkins in people's yards.

Zoe is my dog, and she is white and brown. Zoe knows how to do a lot of tricks. Zoe can speak when you ask her to, and she can shake your hand. Zoe will also give you a kiss when you ask her. I don know many dogs that can do these things.

**12. What is the main idea of the passage? Circle the correct answer choice.**

    Ⓐ  Zoe is my dog.
    Ⓑ  Zoe can give kisses.
    Ⓒ  Zoe is smart.
    Ⓓ  Zoe only knows a few tricks.

Jamie, please come home soon. I miss you when you are away and I am unhappy when you aren here. I have missed your incredible cooking while you've been gone.

**13. What is the main idea of the passage? Circle the correct answer choice.**

    Ⓐ  Jamie made the narrator unhappy.
    Ⓑ  Jamie is a good cook.
    Ⓒ  Jamie is away on vacation.
    Ⓓ  Jamie, I miss you.

# Chapter 2

## Lesson 3: Development of Ideas

*Before answering questions related to this standard, let us understand the meaning of the terms "Main idea Or Theme", "Inference", "Summary" and "Characters".*

**Main Idea Or Theme:** It is the main thought or message being conveyed about the topic. To figure out the main idea, ask yourself: What is being said about the person, thing, or idea (the topic). The main idea is usually the first sentence of the passage. The rest of the passage usually has the supporting ideas and details.

**Inference:** This is a conclusion reached by a reader after reading the information in a passage. The reader uses the information in the passage to reach this conclusion on his/her own; it has not been stated by the author.

**Summary:** to restate the main points or events in an argument or proposal of an idea, usually in a brief, concise manner.

**Character(s):** The actions and thoughts and emotions of the main (major) character(s) have the most influence and are most important to the plot. There may be other less important characters (known as minor or secondary characters) in the story, but they will have less influence on the plot.

Answering the questions below will help you Summarize the text

1. Who is the main character?
2. What did the character want?
3. What was the problem?
4. How did the character try to solve the problem?
5. What was the resolution?

You can scan the QR code given below or use the url to access additional EdSearch resources including videos and mobile apps related to *Development of Ideas*.

## *Development of Ideas*

| URL | QR Code |
|---|---|
| http://www.lumoslearning.com/a/rl62 |  |

always try to do what I have promised to do. If I say I will arrive at 5:15, I try to be there at 5:15. I don't lie or deliberately withhold information. I don't try to trick or confuse others. My friends trust me with their secrets, and I don't tell them to anyone else. I understand that you are looking for a trustworthy employee.

**1. Select the concluding sentence that most completely summarizes the argument in the passage.**

Ⓐ If you are looking for an employee who doesn't lie, then you should hire me.
Ⓑ If you are looking for an employee who needs to be at work at 5:15, then you should hire me.
Ⓒ If you are looking for a trustworthy person, you should hire me.
Ⓓ I believe I would make a very good employee and would love to be considered for a position at your company.

If I am chosen to be class president, I will represent you on the Student Council. I will listen to your requests and be sure that they are heard. I will show up for meetings. I will try to make our school a better place.

**2. Select the concluding sentence that most completely summarizes the argument in the passage.**

Ⓐ If you vote for me, I will be a good class president.
Ⓑ I am a good leader.
Ⓒ I will work towards scrapping exams.
Ⓓ The food in the cafeteria is awful.

Cats do not require as much attention as dogs. Dogs love you, and they want you to love them back. Cats are independent creatures. They don't need to be petted all the time. If you go on vacation for a few days, your dog may get lonely and refuse to eat, but your cat won't care.

**3. Select the concluding sentence that most completely summarizes the argument in the passage.**

Ⓐ If you really want a pet, it would be a good idea to get a cat and a dog.
Ⓑ If you don't have a lot of time to care for a pet, a dog is a better choice for you than a cat.
Ⓒ Vacations are a good idea if you have a cat as a pet.
Ⓓ If you don't have a lot of time to care for a pet, a cat is a better choice for you than a dog.

## 4. Choose the best possible supporting detail to most accurately complete the statements.

1. The beach is a perfect place to take a vacation.
2. I love to laze around on the sands.
3. _____
4. That is why I love to take a vacation at the beach.

    Ⓐ I love the smell of sea water.
    Ⓑ I hate the smell of sea water.
    Ⓒ Starfish are so cool.
    Ⓓ I like to see aircraft fly.

## 5. Choose the best possible supporting detail to most accurately complete the statements.

1. Christmas is everybody's favorite holiday.
2. One gets to do a lot of shopping.
3. _____.
4. That is why everybody loves Christmas.

    Ⓐ Christmas break is boring because you don't get to see your school friends every day.
    Ⓑ The school gives a lot of homework to do over the holidays.
    Ⓒ Decorating the Christmas tree is a lot of work.
    Ⓓ There's a spirit of giving.

One evening, long after most people had gone to bed, a friend and I were making our way merril
back home through the silent and almost deserted streets. We had been to a musical show and wer
talking about the actor we had seen and heard in it.

"That show made him a star overnight," said my friend about one of the actors. "He was completel
unknown before, and now thousands of teenagers send him chocolates and love letters through th
mail."

"I thought he was quite good," I said, "but not worth thousands of love letters daily. As a matter o
fact, one of his songs gave me pain."

"Which was that?" my friend asked. "Sing to me." I burst into a parody of the song.

"Be quiet for heaven's sake!" My friend gave me an astonished look. "You'll give everybody a frigh
and wake people up for miles around."

"Never mind," I said, intoxicated with the sound of my own voice. "I don't care. Why does it matter?

And I went on singing the latest tunes at the top of my voice. Presently there came behind us the sound of heavy footsteps, and before you could say "Jack Robinson," a policeman was standing in front of me, his notebook open, and a determined look on his face.

"Excuse me, sir," he said. "You have a remarkable voice if I may say so. Who taught you to sing? I'd very much like to find someone who can give my daughter singing lessons. Would you be kind enough to tell me your name and address? Then my wife or I can drop you a line and discuss the matter."

**After reading the story, enter the details in the map below. This will help you answer the question with ease.**

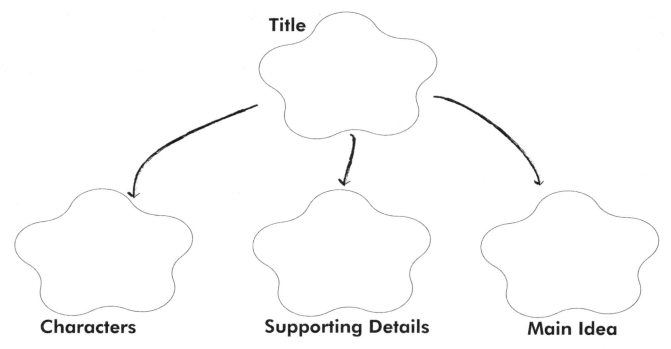

**6. Choose the best title for the above passage.**

- Ⓐ  The Singer
- Ⓑ  A Pleasant Surprise
- Ⓒ  The Musical Show
- Ⓓ  The Policeman

The sky was dark and overcast. It had been raining all night long, and there was no sign of it stopping. I thought that my Sunday would be ruined. As it poured outside, I settled down by the window to watch the rain. The park opposite my house looked even more green and fresh than usual. The branches of the tall trees swayed so hard in the strong wind that I thought they would break. A few children were splashing about in the mud puddles and having a wonderful time. I wished I could join them too! There were very few people out on the road and those who were hurried on their way, wrapped in raincoats and carrying umbrellas.

My mother announced that lunch was ready. It was piping hot and very welcoming in the damp weather. We spent the afternoon listening to music and to the downpour outside.

In the evening, we chatted and made paper boats that we meant to sail in the stream of water outside. It was not a bad day, after all!

**After reading the story, enter the details in the map below. This will help you answer the question with ease.**

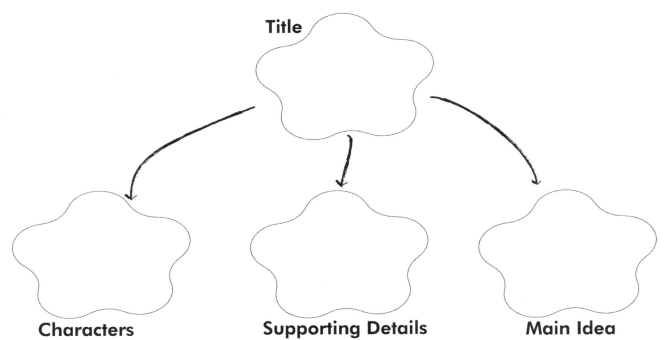

**Title**

**Characters**          **Supporting Details**          **Main Idea**

**7. What detail in the above passage tells us that it was a cloudy day?**

    Ⓐ  The sky was dark and overcast.
    Ⓑ  It had been raining all night long.
    Ⓒ  A few children were splashing about in the mud puddles.
    Ⓓ  The park opposite my house looked even more green and fresh.

The girls went to the park to play on the swings as they did each day. Their mothers always told them never to talk to strangers and always stick together. No one should walk home alone.

**8. What message did the girls get from their mothers?**

Ⓐ Stay together and stay away from strangers.
Ⓑ Only walk home alone if there is no one else to talk with you.
Ⓒ Be friendly to anyone you meet.
Ⓓ Enjoy the park and the people.

Suzanne and her brother always helped out at the shelter. They gave out food to people who would otherwise be hungry. They also gave out blankets, clothes, and jackets. Suzanne and her brother did this twice a month. When they gave these people food, blankets, clothes, and jackets, their faces lit up and they couldn't say thank you enough times.

**9. Which statement indicates the primary message?**

Ⓐ It is always nice and rewarding to help others.
Ⓑ Giving others blankets, clothes, and food can change their lives.
Ⓒ Giving people food will allow them to not go hungry.
Ⓓ Helping others always involves giving blankets.

Allison went to swim practice and worked very hard to try and perfect her flip turn. A flip turn is a turn where you flip underwater and turn to go back in the direction that you came from. Allison practiced 1 hour before school and 3 hours after school each day. On the weekends she practiced 5 hours a day! Allison thought she would never get the flip turn down right, but she practiced and practiced. Finally, after two weeks straight of practicing, she nailed it.

**10. Which statement indicates the primary message?**

Ⓐ If you practice less than two weeks, you won't accomplish your goal.
Ⓑ Only practice on the weekends.
Ⓒ Keep trying and don't give up.
Ⓓ Keep trying, but give up if you get too tired.

# Excerpt from Arabian Nights, Aladdin

**Read the below passage and answer the questions.**

After these words, the magician drew a ring off his finger, and put it on one of Aladdin's, telling him that it was a preservative against all evil, while he should observe what he had prescribed to him. After this instruction he said: "Go down boldly, child, and we shall both be rich all our lives."

Aladdin jumped into the cave, descended the steps, and found the three halls just as the African magician had described. He went through them with all the precaution the fear of death could inspire, crossed the garden without stopping, took down the lamp from the niche, threw out the wick and the liquor, and, as the magician had desired, put it in his vestband. But as he came down from the terrace, he stopped in the garden to observe the fruit, which he only had a glimpse of in crossing it. All the trees were loaded with extraordinary fruit, of different colors on each tree. Some bore fruit entirely white, and some clear and transparent as crystal; some pale red, and others deeper; some green, blue, and purple, and others yellow: in short, there were fruits of all colors. The white were pearls; the clear and transparent, diamonds; the deep red, rubies; the green, emeralds; the blue, turquoises; the purple, amethysts; and those that were of yellow cast, sapphires. Aladdin was altogether ignorant of their worth, and would have preferred figs and grapes, or any other fruits. But though he took them only for colored glass of little value, yet he was so pleased with the variety of the colors and the beauty and extraordinary size of the seeming fruit, that he resolved to gather some of every sort; and accordingly filled the two new purses his uncle had bought for him with his clothes. Some he wrapped up in the skirts of his vest, which was of silk, large and full, and he crammed his bosom as full as it could hold.

Aladdin, having thus loaded himself with riches, returned through the three halls with the same precaution, made all the haste he could, that he might not make his uncle wait, and soon arrived at the mouth of the cave, where the African magician expected him with the utmost impatience. As soon as Aladdin saw him, he cried out: "Pray, uncle, lend me your hand, to help me out." "Give me the lamp first," replied the magician; "it will be troublesome to you." "Indeed, uncle," answered Aladdin, "I cannot now; it is not troublesome to me: but I will as soon as I am up." The African magician was so obstinate, that he would have the lamp before he would help him up; and Aladdin, who had encumbered himself so much with his fruit that he could not well get at it, refused to give it to him till he was out of the cave. The African magician, provoked at this obstinate refusal, flew into a passion, threw a little of his incense into the fire, which he had taken care to keep in, and no sooner pronounced two magical words, than the stone which had closed the mouth of the cave moved into its place, with the earth over it in the same manner as it lay at the arrival of the magician and Aladdin.

## 11. The ring was a _____ against all evil. Write your answer in the box below.

# Writing Task 1

**12. Writing Situation:** The park in your area has only one tennis court. It is always crowded and one has to wait at least two hours before getting a chance to play.

**Writing Task:** Write a persuasive letter to your mayor requesting more tennis courts in your area. In your letter, be sure to describe the situation and explain the reasons why you need more tennis courts.

## Chapter 2

## Lesson 4: Summary of Text

**Before answering the questions, it is important to understand the meaning of Summary and Characters.**

**Summary:** to restate the main points or events in an argument or proposal of an idea, usually in a brief, concise manner.

**Character(s):** The actions and thoughts and emotions of the main (major) character(s) have the most influence and are most important to the plot. There may be other less important characters (known as minor or secondary characters) in the story, but they will have less influence on the plot.

Answering the questions below will help you Summarize the text

1. Who is the main character?
2. What did the character want?
3. What was the problem?
4. How did the character try to solve the problem?
5. What was the resolution?

**You can scan the QR code given below or use the url to access additional EdSearch resources including videos and mobile apps related to *Summary of Text*.**

 **Search**     *Summary of Text*

| URL | QR Code |
| --- | --- |
| http://www.lumoslearning.com/a/rl62 |  |

One evening, long after most people had gone to bed, a friend and I were making our way merrily back home through the silent and almost deserted streets. We had been to a musical show and were talking about the actor we had seen and heard in it.

"That show made him a star overnight," said my friend about one of the actors. "He was completely unknown before, and now thousands of teenagers send him chocolates and love letters through the mail."

"I thought he was quite good," I said, "but not worth thousands of love letters daily. As a matter of fact, one of his songs gave me pain."

"What was that?" my friend asked. "Sing to me." I burst into a parody of the song.

"Be quiet for heaven's sake!" My friend gave me an astonished look. "You'll give everybody a fright and wake people up for miles around."

"Never mind," I said, intoxicated with the sound of my own voice. "I don't care. How does it matter?"

And I went on singing the latest tunes at the top of my voice.

Presently there came behind us the sound of heavy footsteps, and before you could say "Jack Robinson," a policeman was standing in front of me, his notebook open, and a determined look on his face.

"Excuse me, sir," he said. "You have a remarkable voice if I may say so. Who taught you to sing? I'd very much like to find someone who can give my daughter singing lessons. Would you be kind enough to tell me your name and address? Then my wife or I can drop you a line and discuss the matter."

**After reading the story, enter the details in the map below. This will help you answer the question with ease.**

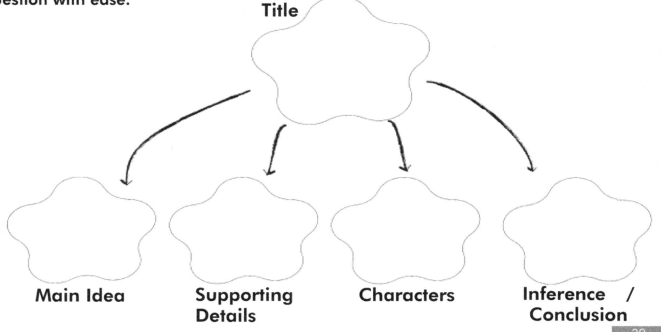

**Title**

**Main Idea**          **Supporting Details**          **Characters**          **Inference / Conclusion**

## 1. What probably happened at the end of the story?

&#9398;   Both the friends went home and had dinner
&#9399;   The writer gave the policeman his name and address.
&#9400;   The policeman arrested both the friends
&#9401;   They went to see another musical show

Thomas is on the football team, the basketball team, and the hockey team. He even likes to run when he has free time.

## 2. By reading this you can conclude that _____?

Michael decided to climb a ladder to get his frisbee that landed on the roof. His father always told him to be careful when using a ladder because ladders were dangerous. Michael put on his bike helmet, asked his friend to hold the ladder, and put one hand in front of the other while climbing, never letting go of the ladder.

## 3. What can you conclude about climbing a ladder?

&#9398; It is a lot of fun.
&#9399; It is easy if you know what to do.
&#9400; You should only climb a ladder if you are over 13 years old.
&#9401; It can be very dangerous.

On the first day of school, there are many supplies that a student needs. Every student needs notebook, pencils, pens, highlighters, and the most important, a calendar.

## 4. What sentence below most closely agrees with these sentences?

&#9398; All of these items help a student stay organized throughout the year.
&#9399; These items are only helpful for students who enjoy math.
&#9400; These items are expensive, so only buy a few of them.
&#9401; You may not need all these items to stay organized.

It is great to have a younger sibling. Some people may think it is annoying, but those people don't realize the benefits of having a younger sibling. First, a younger sibling can do your chores for you, so you don't get in trouble. Second, they can feed the animals, so you don't have to do that. Third, they can actually be fun to play with when you are stuck at home on a snow day.

**5. What can you summarize from this passage?**

   Ⓐ  It is great to have younger siblings.
   Ⓑ  Younger siblings are annoying.
   Ⓒ  You only want a sibling to be older than you.
   Ⓓ  Being an only child is the best.


Ryan earned money each week from doing chores around the house. His mother always told him that it was his money, but he should not spend it on useless things. Ryan decided to take $5.00 out of his piggy bank and went into the candy store. He looked at all the different types of candy and spent all of his $5.00.

**6. What is the most important message in this passage?**

   Ⓐ  Ryan loves candy.
   Ⓑ  Ryan begged for his money.
   Ⓒ  Ryan had a green piggy bank.
   Ⓓ  Ryan shared his candy with his friends.


The little girl got to pick out new furniture and decorate her room. She really liked the white bed and dresser. She decided to paint her walls pink and get a pink carpet. She was so excited to be getting a new room!

**7. What can you summarize about this little girl?**

   Ⓐ  She had always had a room to herself.
   Ⓑ  She was excited to redo her room the way she wanted.
   Ⓒ  She wanted to paint her room purple.
   Ⓓ  Her mother wasn't happy with her decisions.

Damon was moving to another state on the other side of the country. Along the way as his family drove, they stopped in Illinois, Idaho, and South Dakota; none of the towns they stopped in were like his hometown. When he arrived in his new hometown, he was excited to be living in a different state.

**8. What can you summarize about this passage?**

Ⓐ   Damon was moving to South Dakota.
Ⓑ   Damon guessed that his new hometown would not be like his old hometown, but was excited to be moving anyway.
Ⓒ   Damon did not want to stop in other states along the way.
Ⓓ   Damon was moving to Illinois.

The girl stood looking out the window
No one was out there, not even an animal.
The wind blew softly and rain started to fall.
The clouds rolled in and the thunder came.
The girl felt like she was looking through the window into her own mood.

**9. Based on this poem, what answer best describes the girl's mood?**

Ⓐ   The girl liked to be alone.
Ⓑ   She was scared of the rain.
Ⓒ   The girl was sad and unhappy.
Ⓓ   The girl was excited.

A boy embarked on a journey
Not knowing where he would end up.
He packed his things and headed out West.
It took him days and days to get to where he was going.
He was nervous and scared about what may be out there.
When the boy arrived, he wasn't sure if he was ready for what was to come.

**10. What was the boy doing?**

Ⓐ   The boy was moving and starting a new life.
Ⓑ   The boy was going to become an actor.
Ⓒ   The boy was going to find his long lost brother.
Ⓓ   The boy was going on a vacation.

Once upon a time, four boys lived in the countryside. One boy was very clever, but he did not like books. His name was Good Sense. The other boys were not very clever, but they read every book in the school. When they became grown men, they decided to go out into the world to earn their livelihood.

They left home and came to a forest where they halted for the night. When they woke up in the morning, they found the bones of a lion. Three of them, who had learned their books well at school, decided to make a lion out of the bones.

Good Sense told them, "A lion is a dangerous animal. It will kill us. Don't make a lion." But the three disregarded his advice and started making a lion. Good Sense was very clever. When his friends were busy making the lion, he climbed up a tree to save himself. No sooner had the three young men created the lion and gave it life, than it pounced upon them and ate them up. Good Sense climbed down the tree and went home very sadly.

**After reading the story, enter the details in the map below. This will help you answer the questions with ease.**

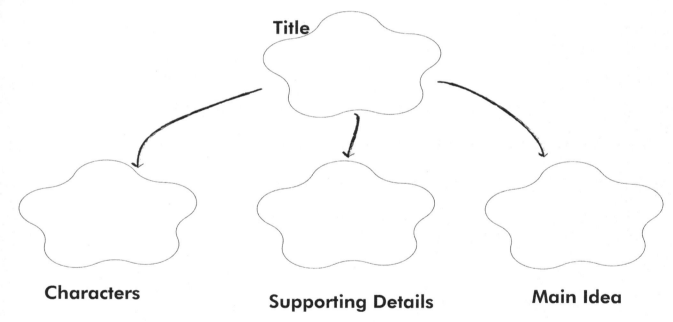

**Title**

**Characters**          **Supporting Details**          **Main Idea**

**1. Part A**
   **What can be an appropriate title for the above story?**

   Ⓐ   The Four Friends
   Ⓑ   Good Sense
   Ⓒ   The Lion and the Friends
   Ⓓ   The Men

## 11. Part B
**What is the moral of the story?**

Ⓐ   Listen to a wise person's advice
Ⓑ   Never listen to someone who does not like to read books
Ⓒ   Think before you act
Ⓓ   Both A and C

I'm nobody! Who are you?

I'm nobody! Who are you?
Are you nobody, too?
Then there's a pair of us — don't tell!
They'd banish us; you know!

How dreary to be somebody!
How public like a frog
To tell one's name the livelong day
To an admiring bog!

-Emily Dickinson

Emily Dickinson is a well- known American poet who was born in the 1800's.

## 12. What do you think she is talking about in this poem?

Ⓐ   She feels as if people do not see or notice her, and she likes it that way.
Ⓑ   She wants to be a frog.
Ⓒ   She doesn't like being not noticed and does want to be important.
Ⓓ   She is not making any comparisons in this poem.

# Chapter 2

## Lesson 5: Characters Responses and Changes

*Publisher's note: Theatrical plays, dance compositions, books and musical compositions use scenes, chapters and stanzas respectively to deliver their themes or stories. Scenes, chapters and stanzas divide the stories and performances into separate parts in which characters, settings, events, melodies and choruses are introduced and re-introduced. Dividing these performances into separate parts holds the audiences' attention, creating variety and interest. While each part is unique, it still relates and complements the overall production; each part makes up the structure of the overall production. The play Les Misérables is an example of how individual parts (scenes) fit together to form the entire play.*

*Note: In the example below, the text that is in italics (looks just like this note) are comments you might make in writing what is required by the standard . The plot of the story, as presented in the example, unfolds as a series of episodes presented in the order in which they occur.*

*Let us understand the concept with an example.*

### Les Misérables

The story begins as the peasant Jean Valjean, just released from 19 years' imprisonment, is turned away by innkeepers because his yellow passport marks him as a former convict. He sleeps on the street, angry and bitter.

A benevolent local priest gives him shelter. At night, Valjean runs off with the priest's silverware (remember that Valjean went to prison for stealing, so it looks like he has not changed), but when the police capture Valjean, the priest lies to protect him and tells him that his life has been spared for God, and that he should use money from the silverware to make an honest man of himself. But although Valjean broods over the priest's advice, he steals a coin from a 12-year-old boy. His theft is reported to the authorities and Valjean hides as they search for him because if apprehended he will be returned to jail for life as a repeat offender.

Six years pass and Valjean, using an alias, has become a wealthy factory owner and mayor of the town. Walking down the street, he sees a man pinned under the wheels of a cart. When no one volunteers to help, he decides to rescue the man himself by crawling underneath the cart and lifting it to free him (he shows he is capable of compassion, and now wealthy, he apparently does not want to steal anymore). The town's police inspector, Inspector Javert, who was a guard at the prison during Valjean's incarceration, becomes suspicious of the mayor after witnessing this remarkable feat of strength. He has known only one other man, a convict named Jean Valjean, who could accomplish it. Note: This past relationship between Valjean and Javert has now been rekindled.

Years earlier in Paris, a woman named Fantine was very much in love with a man with whom she had a child, but the man left her to fend for herself and her daughter Cosette. She arrives in the town in which Valjean is the mayor. In order to work, Fantine leaves Cosette in the care of the Thénardiers, a corrupt innkeeper and his selfish, cruel wife. Fantine ends up working at Valjean's factory. She is later fired from her job at Valjean's factory because of the discovery of her daughter, who was born out of wedlock. Fantine is attacked in the street and arrested by Javert who sentences her to prison but Valjean intervenes (another encounter between these two men) and takes the ill woman to the hospital and promises Fantine that he will bring Cosette to her. But Fantine dies before this happens. Note: And thus another connection among characters is created: Valjean, Fantine, Cosette, Javert and the Thénardiers. Javert is now an enemy of Valjean and tries to arrange his capture, but Valjean escapes and searches for Cosette who he promised Fantine he would take care of.

Valjean returns to his home city and finds Cosette alone and walks with her to the inn. He orders a meal and observes how the Thénardiers abuse her, while pampering their own daughters Éponine and Azelma. The next morning, Valjean informs the Thénardiers that he wants to take Cosette with him. Madame Thénardier immediately accepts, while Thénardier pretends to love Cosette and be concerned for her welfare, reluctant to give her up. Valjean pays off the Thénardiers, and he and Cosette leave the inn.

Valjean and Cosette flee to Paris, where he and Cosette live happily. However, Javert discovers Valjean's lodgings there a few months later. Valjean takes Cosette and they try to escape from Javert. They soon find shelter in a convent with the help of the man whom Valjean once rescued from being crushed under a cart and who has become the convent's gardener. Note: the past relationship between the man Valjean rescued and Valjean is rekindled. Valjean also becomes a gardener and Cosette becomes a student at the convent school.

Publisher's Note: The story continues, with new relationships, such as those between a young man named Marius and Cosette, in spite of the extreme jealousy of Éponine, Thenardier's daughter. Yes, the Thenardiers enter into Valjean's life again, as does Javert, and the French Revolution draws in Marius and Valjean and Cosette. But we're going to end the story here because our intent was not to give a synopsis of the entire play but to demonstrate how a series of individual scenes fit together to provide the overall structure of the play (and in a similar manner, a book or a dance performance or a musical performance), as required by the standard above.

You can scan the QR code given below or use the url to access additional EdSearch resources including videos and mobile apps related to *Characters Responses and Changes.*

 Search

# *Characters Responses and Changes*

| URL | QR Code |
|---|---|
| http://www.lumoslearning.com/a/rl63 |  |

One evening, long after most people had gone to bed, a friend and I were making our way merri[l] back home through the silent and almost deserted streets. We had been to a musical show and wer[e] talking about the actor we had seen and heard in it.

"That show made him a star overnight," said my friend about one of the actors. "He was complete[ly] unknown before, and now thousands of teenagers send him chocolates and love letters through th[e] mail."

"I thought he was quite good," I said, "but not worth thousands of love letters daily. As a matter [of] fact, one of his songs gave me pain."

"Which was that?" my friend asked. "Sing to me." I burst into a parody of the song.

"Be quiet for heaven's sake!" My friend gave me an astonished look. "You'll give everybody a frigh[t] and wake people up for miles around."

"Never mind," I said, intoxicated with the sound of my own voice. "I don't care. Why does it matter?"

And I went on singing the latest tunes at the top of my voice. Presently there came behind us the soun[d] of heavy footsteps, and before you could say "Jack Robinson," a policeman was standing in front [of] me, his notebook open, and a determined look on his face.

"Excuse me, sir," he said. "You have a remarkable voice if I may say so. Who taught you to sing[?] I'd very much like to find someone who can give my daughter singing lessons. Would you be kin[d] enough to tell me your name and address? Then my wife or I can drop you a line and discuss th[e] matter."

**After reading the story, enter the details in the map below. This will help you answer th[e] questions with ease.**

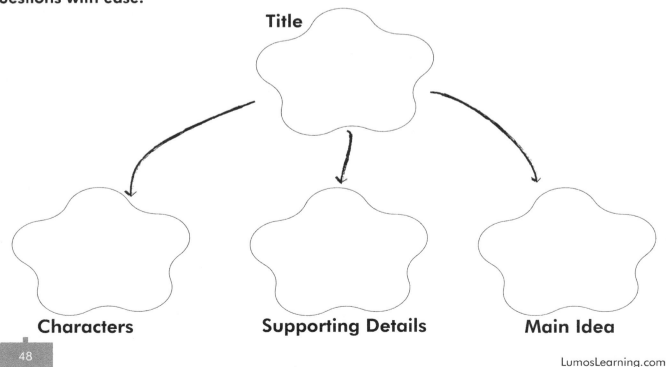

**1. Who are the three characters in the above passage?**

Ⓐ the writer, the writer's friend, and the actor
Ⓑ the writer, the writer's friend, and the singer
Ⓒ the neighbors, the policeman, and his friend
Ⓓ the writer, the writer's friend, and the policeman

**2. Who were the writer and his friend referring to when they were talking and said "his songs"?**

Ⓐ their neighbors
Ⓑ the policeman
Ⓒ the actor who sang in the musical show
Ⓓ the friend

The sky was dark and overcast. It had been raining all night long, and there was no sign of it stopping. I thought that my Sunday would be ruined. As it poured outside, I settled down by the window to watch the rain. The park opposite my house looked even more green and fresh than usual. The branches of the tall trees swayed so hard in the strong wind that I thought they would break. A few children were splashing about in the mud puddles and having a wonderful time. I wished I could join them too! There were very few people out on the road and those who were hurried on their way, wrapped in raincoats and carrying umbrellas.

My mother announced that lunch was ready. It was piping hot and very welcoming in the damp weather. We spent the afternoon listening to music and to the downpour outside.

In the evening, we chatted and made paper boats that we meant to sail in the stream of water outside. It was not a bad day, after all!

After reading the story, enter the details in the map below. This will help you answer the questions with ease.

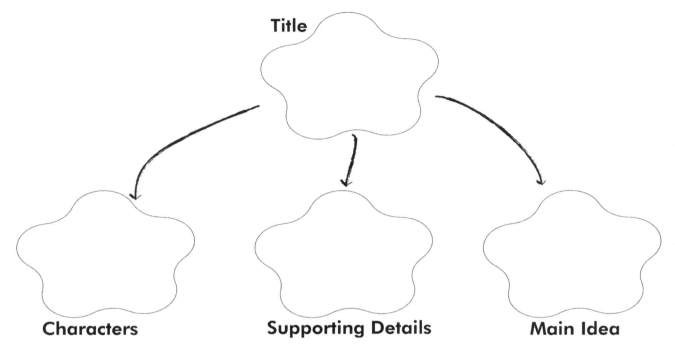

3. Who is the main character in the above passage?

Ⓐ The rain
Ⓑ The writer's mom
Ⓒ The writer
Ⓓ The wind

4. The character in a story who dominates is a _____.

Ⓐ minor character
Ⓑ major character
Ⓒ supporting character
Ⓓ Joker

Sally woke up earlier than she expected one morning. Something wasn't right. She then realized what had awakened her. It was an unfamiliar sound. She listened closely and realized that the sound was coming from outside. Climbing out of her bed, she slipped into her robe and slippers and went to the window. Looking out, she soon spotted a small kitten under the tree that stood outside her window. She stood, staring at the helpless creature. It didn't move. It soon spotted her and meowed, as if it were calling out to her.

Sally left her room and found her mother in the kitchen. She excitedly told her mom about the kitten. "I am going outside to get the poor little thing," she told her mother.

"I'll go with you," her mom replied. Together they walked into the backyard. The kitten was still there waiting for them. Sally picked it up in her arms. The little kitten felt so soft and cuddly. She had always wanted a kitten and wondered if her mother would allow her to keep him. Her mother decided to first feed the kitten. She also decided to make a few calls to see where he came from. The kitten certainly needed a home. Sally became more hopeful that she would be able to keep the kitten.

**After reading the story, enter the details in the map below. This will help you answer the questions with ease.**

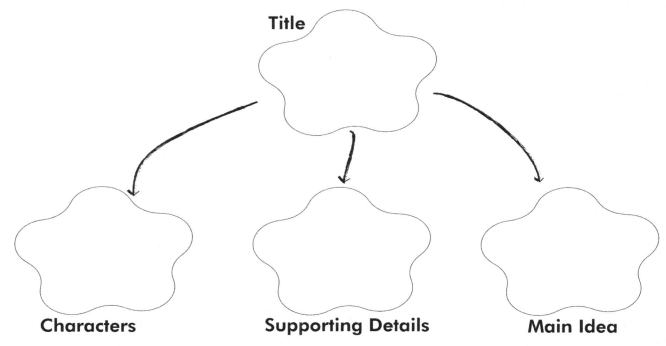

5. The characters in the story are _____.

Ⓐ the kitten
Ⓑ the mother
Ⓒ Sally
Ⓓ All of the above

**6. The main character in a story is usually known as the _____.**

- Ⓐ Protagonist
- Ⓑ Antagonist
- Ⓒ One who saves everyone
- Ⓓ The one who messes everything up

**7. The descriptions given by an author about the character's personality, habits, like and dislikes are called?**

- Ⓐ Character style
- Ⓑ Character flaws
- Ⓒ Character traits
- Ⓓ Character ideas

Having to start at a new school didn't worry Jane at all; she was ready for anything.

**8. A character trait of Jane is _____.**

- Ⓐ Easy-going
- Ⓑ Shy
- Ⓒ Scared
- Ⓓ Nervous

Realizing his son's dog was still in the burning building, the dad ran back into the building.

**9. A character trait of the father is _____.**

- Ⓐ Nervous
- Ⓑ Scared
- Ⓒ Carefree
- Ⓓ Selfless

Ever since Greg was little, he always liked to take things apart. He took apart his sister's dolls, too apart all his trucks and cars, and even took apart his parents' telephone to see how it worked.

**10. A character trait of Greg is_____?**

- Ⓐ Destructive
- Ⓑ Angry
- Ⓒ Curious
- Ⓓ Mean

**11. Why did the magician get angry with Aladdin on his return?
Write your answer in the box below.**

[ ]

# Increase Your Vocabulary

**Additional vocabulary to add:**

**Caveat emptor**- [**kav**-ee-aht**emp**-tawr] Latin, noun, let the buyer beware. The person who is purchasing something is responsible for noting any problems with their purchase, unless a warranty is made.

**Carte blanche**-[kart blahnSH] French, noun, complete freedom to act as one wishes thinks is best. Full discretionary power.

**Tete a tete**-[ 2 is also] French, noun, a personal conversation between two people. Adjective, face to face, private. Adverb, in private.

**Alfresco**-[]   Italian,  adj, adv, open air, outdoors.

**Pas de deaux** - [pa de du] French,noun, a dance duet in which 2 dancers perform ballet steps.

**Bon appetite** - [bawna-pey-tee] French, true meaning is that may you enjoy your meal; however, in France it is a saying that the host announces to let the guests know it is time to begin eating.

**Quid pro quo** - [kwid]  Latin, noun,something given or received for something else.

**Alma mater**-  **Latin, noun, an institution, school, university, college, where one has graduated from.**

Practice questions and explanations.

In the English language, numerous words are derived from other languages and used frequently in written English. These words have become common place to most people.  However, some may be unfamiliar and it is necessary to describe their origin for greater understanding of their meaning.

**Sample sentences to reinforce understanding of derived meanings:**

When purchasing a couch at the antique auction, Mr Willis took note of <u>caveat emptor</u> before agreeing to the sale.

We had <u>carte blanche</u> when it came to choosing our fishing site, guide, and schooner at the hotel in the Caribbean.

It was obvious that the couple was engaged in a <u>tete a tete</u> as they huddled in the corner booth.

The group enjoyed their time dining <u>alfresco</u> on the San Antonio River Walk in San Antonio, Texas.

The dancers had perfected the <u>pas de deaux</u> while performing Sleeping Beauty at the local theatre.

As usual, Maryann announced "<u>Bon appetite</u>" as we began our first-course appetizers at the French restaurant.

It was obvious to all who attended the hearing that <u>quid pro quo</u> was applicable in the case in front of the jury.

Scott and Sarah were boisterous and could be heard above the entire crowd as they sang during their 20th-year reunion at their <u>alma mater</u> in Dayton, Ohio.

**12. Look at the words given below.**

1. graduated from
2. a private meeting between 2 people
3. dance step with 2 people
4. contract made between parties for services
5. full discretionary power
6. salutation to eat
7. outside
8. buyer beware

**Match the following vocabulary with its meaning from the list of words given above.**

| | |
|---|---|
| Alma mater | ——————— |
| Pas de deaux | ——————— |
| Carte blanche | ——————— |
| Bon appetite | ——————— |
| Tete a tete | ——————— |
| Quid pro quo | ——————— |
| Alfresco | ——————— |
| Caveat emptor | ——————— |

(Tay duh tate)

# Chapter 2

## Lesson 6: Figurative Words and Phrases

**Definitions:**

**1. Figurative:** language is language where the meaning is different from the literal (primary or strict or dictionary) meaning. Another way of defining this term is: using language that has another meaning besides its normal definition. Examples of figurative language: simile, metaphor, personification, and alliteration.

**2. Connotative:** language suggests an associated or secondary meaning of a word or expression in addition to its primary meaning. Examples: a puppy or kitten connotes cuteness; a hurricane warning connotes danger and the need to take shelter.

Let us understand the concept with an example.

Faster than fairies, faster than witches,
Bridges and houses, hedges and ditches;
And charging along like troops in a battle,
All through the meadows the horses and cattle:
All of the sights of the hill and the plain,
Fly as thick as driving rain;
And ever again, in the wink of an eye,
Painted stations whistle by.

Here is a child who clambers and scrambles,
All by himself and gathering brambles;
Here is a tramp who stands and gazes,
And there is the green for stinging the daisies!
Here is a cart run away in the road,
Lumping along with man and load;
And here is a mill and there is a river,
Each a glimpse and gone forever!

By R.L. Stevenson

**This is what you might write.**

This is a poem and it has rhyming, which are two examples of figurative language. It also contains similes. One is comparing charging horses and cattle to troops in battle. Another is the hill and the plain flying by thick as driving rain.

The poem also uses imagery, which is a figurative language technique used to represent objects, actions, and ideas in such a way that it appeals to our physical senses. Nearly every line of the poem describes scenery in such a way that each reader can paint a mental picture.

The poem is written in such a way that the reader senses there is some connotative meaning hidden behind the imagery of the scenery. Descriptive phrases like "Painted stations whistle by," "faster than fairies, faster than witches (on brooms?)", and the animals charging along, and the phrase "Each glimpse and gone forever!" The alert reader will probably figure out that the poem is written as if the poet was viewing the scenery from a rapidly moving train.

**You can scan the QR code given below or use the url to access additional EdSearch resources including videos and mobile apps related to *Figurative Words and Phrases*.**

 **Search**

## *Figurative Words and Phrases*

| URL | QR Code |
|---|---|
| http://www.lumoslearning.com/a/rl64 |  |

**1. Choose the sentence below that is closest in meaning to the figurative expression.**

Edgar was dead to the world when we got home.

    Ⓐ  Edgar was asleep when we got home.
    Ⓑ  Edgar was not moving or breathing.
    Ⓒ  Edgar had a head injury and was unconscious.
    Ⓓ  Edgar was not at home.

**2. Choose the sentence below that is closest in meaning to the figurative expression.**

You'd better go home; you're in hot water.

    Ⓐ  You'd better go home; you're in trouble
    Ⓑ  You'd better go home; you'll find hot water there.
    Ⓒ  You'd better go home; you are sweating.
    Ⓓ  You'd better go home and drink hot water.

**3. Choose the sentence below that is closest in meaning to the figurative expression.**

He put all the papers in the circular file.

    Ⓐ  He put the papers in the wastebasket.
    Ⓑ  He rolled up all the papers.
    Ⓒ  He put the papers in the round file cabinet.
    Ⓓ  He put the papers on the circular table.

**4. Choose the word below that, completes the figurative expression.**

He works like a _____.

    Ⓐ  Lion
    Ⓑ  Dog
    Ⓒ  Parrot
    Ⓓ  Cat

**5. Choose the word below that, completes the figurative expression.**

He is as stubborn as a _____.

    Ⓐ  Mule
    Ⓑ  Cow
    Ⓒ  Baby
    Ⓓ  Ice

**6. Choose the sentence below that is closest in meaning to the figurative expression.**

The secretary had a mountain of paper work. _____.

- Ⓐ The secretary was dealing with paper art
- Ⓑ The secretary had a large amount of work
- Ⓒ The secretary had to run around a lot
- Ⓓ The secretary had to meet a lot of people

**7. Complete the sentence below so that it is closest in meaning to the figurative expression.**

His room is a train wreck. It is _____.

- Ⓐ full of toy trains
- Ⓑ well organized
- Ⓒ a mess
- Ⓓ well laid out

**8. Complete the sentence below so that it is closest in meaning to the figurative expression.**

He is a star. He _____.

- Ⓐ he loves soccer
- Ⓑ wants to be an astronomer
- Ⓒ acts in films
- Ⓓ is very good at what he does

**9. Complete the sentence below so that it is closest in meaning to the figurative expression.**

She is my rock. She always _____ me.

- Ⓐ puts me down
- Ⓑ leans on
- Ⓒ criticizes
- Ⓓ supports

**10. Complete the sentence below so that it is closest in meaning to the figurative expression.**

I feel like a million bucks. I am _____.

- Ⓐ elated
- Ⓑ happy
- Ⓒ discontented
- Ⓓ Both A & B

**1. Choose the sentence below that is closest in meaning to the figurative expression.**

He put his foot in his mouth.

&#9398; He said something funny.
&#9399; He said something difficult to understand.
&#9400; He was sarcastic.
&#9401; He said something he regretted.

**2. Choose the sentence below that is closest in meaning to the figurative expression.**

Don't bug me!

&#9398; Don't bother me.
&#9399; Don't sneak.
&#9400; Don't tell me anything about yourself.
&#9401; Don't try to get the better of me.

**3. Choose the sentence below that is closest in meaning to the figurative expression.**

He quit smoking cold turkey.

&#9398; He quit eating poultry.
&#9399; He quit cooking.
&#9400; He quit smoking suddenly and without help.
&#9401; He quit smoking Turkish cigars.

## Chapter 2

## Lesson 7: Connotative Words and Phrases

You can scan the QR code given below or use the url to access additional EdSearch resource including videos and mobile apps related to *Connotative Words and Phrases.*

 **Connotative Words and Phrases**

| URL | QR Code |
|---|---|
| http://www.lumoslearning.com/a/rl64 |  |

**1. Choose the best word to complete each sentence.**

My friend is very careful about spending money. I admire that, so I call him _____.

   Ⓐ  thrifty
   Ⓑ  stingy
   Ⓒ  miserly
   Ⓓ  selfish

**2. Choose the best word to complete each sentence.**

My friend is very careful about spending money. I don't like that trait, so I call him _____.

   Ⓐ  thrifty
   Ⓑ  stingy
   Ⓒ  rude
   Ⓓ  mean

**3. Choose the best word to complete each sentence.**

I admire the man who jumped on the subway tracks to rescue a stranger. He was certainly _____.

   Ⓐ  foolhardy
   Ⓑ  undecided
   Ⓒ  courageous
   Ⓓ  stupid

Faster than fairies, faster than witches,
Bridges and houses, hedges and ditches,
And charging along like troops in a battle,
All through the meadows the horses and cattle,
All of the sights of the hill and the plain,
Fly as thick as driving rain,
And ever again, in the wink of an eye,
Painted stations whistle by.

Here is a child who clambers and scrambles,
All by himself and gathering brambles;
Here is a tramp who stands and gazes,
And there is the green for stinging the daisies;
Here is a cart run away in the road,

Lumping along with man and load;
And here is a mill and there is a river,
Each a glimpse and gone forever.
-- R. L. STEVENSON

**4. In the above poem what does the word "brambles" mean?**

Ⓐ  people
Ⓑ  crowds of people
Ⓒ  train stations
Ⓓ  prickly blueberry - and blackberry bushes

The girls on the playground were playing hopscotch. They all played together at recess every day. The new girl sat at the corner of the playground by herself, so one of the girls was _____ and asked her if she wanted to join them.

**5. Which word best completes the sentence?**

Ⓐ  Snotty
Ⓑ  Proud
Ⓒ  Friendly
Ⓓ  Clever

Micky and Janie live in a quiet neighborhood and are very sweet and polite. However, the husband and wife are upset by their noisy neighbors.

**6. Which of the following represents what they might say to their neighbors?**

Ⓐ  Hey! Keep quiet over there!
Ⓑ  Hello...would you mind keep the noise level down? We have sleeping children over here.
Ⓒ  How dare you make this much noise when we have sleeping children over here!
Ⓓ  If you don't get quiet in the next 5 minutes, we're calling the cops!

The first aid supplies that were brought after the hurricane were _____. Even after they came, the survivors of the hurricane kept looking for supplies.

**7. Which word best completes the sentence?**

Ⓐ  inadequate
Ⓑ  helpful
Ⓒ  tragic
Ⓓ  important

Skipping school can _____ your future.

**3. What word best fits in the blank?**

Ⓐ effect
Ⓑ help
Ⓒ affect
Ⓓ None of the above

The _____ candidate put his hands high in the sky and pumped his arms with a huge smile on his face.

**9. What word best fits in the blank?**

Ⓐ unhappy
Ⓑ bewildered
Ⓒ victorious
Ⓓ fun

Jackie read the newspaper and found out that there was a twister that hit Alabama and her heart broke for the affected families. The twister wiped out hundreds of houses. This was such a _____ event.

**0. What word best fits in the blank?**

Ⓐ exciting
Ⓑ tragic
Ⓒ unimportant
Ⓓ victorious

The little girl threw her dolls all over her room, took her crayons and drew on the wall of her bedroom, and even pulled the dog's tail.

**1. What word describes this girl's behavior?**

Ⓐ snotty
Ⓑ bratty
Ⓒ nervous
Ⓓ happy

## Chapter 2

### Lesson 8: Meaning of Words and Phrases

You can scan the QR code given below or use the url to access additional EdSearch resource including videos and mobile apps related to *Meaning of Words and Phrases*.

## Meaning of Words and Phrases

| URL | QR Code |
|-----|---------|
| http://www.lumoslearning.com/a/rl64 |  |

"That show made him a star overnight", said my friend about one of the actors. "He was completely unknown before. And now thousands of teenagers send him chocolates and love letters in the mail."

## 1. What does the above paragraph mean?

Ⓐ  that the actor had poor acting skills
Ⓑ  that the actor had come to fame recently
Ⓒ  that nobody likes him now
Ⓓ  none of the above

The forest's sentinel
Glides silently across the hill
And perches in an old pine tree,
A friendly presence his!
No harm can come
From night bird on the prowl.
His cry is mellow,
Much softer than a peacock's call.

Why then this fear of owls
Calling in the night?
If men must speak,
Then owls must hoot-
They have the right.
On me it casts no spell:
Rather, it seems to cry,
"The night is good- all's well, all's well."

-- RUSKIN BOND

## 2. What is the poet talking about in the first stanza?

Ⓐ  how the owl comes out into the night
Ⓑ  how the owl catches its prey
Ⓒ  how the owl is looking into the dark night
Ⓓ  how the owl walks

## 3. What is the poet saying about the owl?

Ⓐ  He is comparing the owl to a sentinel
Ⓑ  He is describing the flight of the owl
Ⓒ  He is saying that the owl is friendly and harmless
Ⓓ  All of the above

The sky was dark and overcast. It had been raining all night long, and there was no sign of it stopping. I thought that my Sunday would be ruined. As it poured outside, I settled down by the window to watch the rain. The park opposite my house looked even more green and fresh than usual. The branches of the tall trees swayed so hard in the strong wind that I thought they would break. A few children were splashing about in the mud puddles and having a wonderful time. I wished I could join them too! There were very few people out on the road and those who were hurried on their way, wrapped in raincoats and carrying umbrellas.

My mother announced that lunch was ready. It was piping hot and very welcoming in the damp weather. We spent the afternoon listening to music and to the downpour outside.

In the evening, we chatted and made paper boats that we meant to sail in the stream of water outside. It was not a bad day, after all!

**4. How does the writer end the passage?**

Ⓐ  With a satisfied tone
Ⓑ  With a sad tone
Ⓒ  With a annoyed tone
Ⓓ  With an excited tone

Androcles was a slave who escaped from his master and fled to the forest. As he was wandering there, he came upon a lion lying down moaning and groaning. Seeing the lion in pain, he removed a huge thorn from the beast's paw. After this incident, they lived together as great friends in the forest. Androcles was eventually arrested and condemned to death in the arena. He would be thrown to a lion that was captured and not given food for several days. The Emperor and his courtiers came to see the spectacle. Androcles was lead to the middle of the arena and so was the hungry lion. The lion roared and rushed towards its victim. But, as soon as he came near Androcles, he recognized him and licked his hands like a friendly dog. Everyone was surprised. The emperor heard the whole story and pardoned Androcles and freed the lion to his native forest.

**5. This story brings out the meaning of _____.**

Ⓐ  Friendship
Ⓑ  Slavery
Ⓒ  Escape
Ⓓ  Hunger

Last week, I fell off my bike and hurt myself badly. I bruised my elbow and sprained my wrist. My injuries would have been worse if I hadn't been wearing my bicycle helmet. My doctor asked me to tell this to all my friends so that they would wear helmets too. I told my teacher, and she asked me to make a public announcement during the school assembly. I had to talk about the accident and how the helmet protected me.

**6. Why was I asked to tell everyone about my accident and mention wearing the helmet?**

Ⓐ  so that everyone understands the benefit of wearing a helmet
Ⓑ  because it made an interesting story
Ⓒ  so that everyone comes to know what a hero I am
Ⓓ  so that helmets can be sold

Life and death were ideal as they crept into the dark world.

**7. What is the mood of this sentence?**

Ⓐ  Ominous
Ⓑ  Tragic
Ⓒ  Dramatic
Ⓓ  Silly

The man was feeble-minded and did not realize when others made fun of him by laughing at him and talking behind his back.

**8. What is the tone of this sentence?**

Ⓐ  Unconcerned
Ⓑ  Upsetting
Ⓒ  Angry
Ⓓ  Rude

My brother comes in my room and hides my dolls,
but my brother plays hide and seek with me.
My brother tells me I'm annoying and should leave his room,
but my brother stands up for me on the playground when someone is mean to me.
My brother plays with his friends and tells me I'm too young to join them,
but my brother plays with me in the snow when we have a snow day.

**9. What is the hidden meaning in the poem?**

Ⓐ  The brother easily gets frustrated with his sibling.
Ⓑ  The brother doesn't want to play with his sibling.
Ⓒ  The brother really loves his sibling.
Ⓓ  The brother likes to play with dolls.

Without you here, I can move forward
Thinking of the past only makes it worse,
Forgetting is the only way to continue on

**10. What is the meaning of the poem?**

Ⓐ  The narrator is angry at someone
Ⓑ  The narrator is moving away
Ⓒ  The narrator wants to think of all the memories
Ⓓ  The narrator wants to move forward; it is too sad to look back

Joe went into school with his clothes on backwards. He even dyed his hair green. He brought a few
magic tricks in and did them for his friends. When he did them, they all laughed.

**11. Based on these sentences, what inference can you make about Joe? Circle the correc
answer choice.**

Ⓐ  Joe is serious.
Ⓑ  Joe is rude.
Ⓒ  Joe is funny.
Ⓓ  Joe is caring.

Samantha was on the track team and was trying to perform her personal best in the high jump. Sh
jumped 4 feet and made it over with ease. She then attempted her personal best at 5 feet, but did no
make it on her first attempt. She tried four more times and, on the fifth try, she made it!

**12. What is the meaning of this passage?**

Ⓐ  Keep trying to perform your personal best even if you fail the first time.
Ⓑ  Only try something five times.
Ⓒ  If you fail to perform your personal best, you may not succeed, even if you try again.
Ⓓ  The faster you run, the higher you can go.

68

# Chapter 2

## Lesson 9: Develop Setting

*Let us understand the concept with an example.*

### The Servant's Escape
By Vivek Krishnaswamy

Late at night when there are people walking around the streets of the city, I lie in my bed hoping that one day I will have the freedom to go out when I want and to get a job outside of the house that I live and work in, with a salary higher than what I am making now.

Today was a typical day around here. It was one o'clock in the afternoon and I was washing the lunch dishes when the mistress of the house walked into the kitchen and said angrily: "Marcos! What is this? What is this? My clothes have been washed but they have not been IRONED!! Do it now or you will be punished!!" So I stopped washing dishes and walked to her room with her dress in my hand, ironed it quickly, then went back to washing dishes. She and the master were always complaining about my work, and rarely complimented me, even though I tried to never disobey them. But there were times when I did not do exactly what they wanted me to do in the exact manner they wanted, and I would get punished with beatings from the gardener. And, I was not allowed to leave the house – I was, in reality, a prisoner.

One night an idea struck me! I looked at the back door and thought: why couldn't I escape from the house through the back door when the family was out, and then come back in before the family returned? I always knew their schedules. While I was out I could look for another job, and if I found one, I would tell the family, and I could leave if they agreed. If they said no, I was doomed; I could just escape but their friends in the police department would track me down and arrest me!

For several weeks I struggled to find a proper job that would give me some time for myself, that also had a place for me to live, and paid a better salary. I finally found what I was looking for. It was a small grocery store where I would help the owner run the store. On the second floor was a small room in which I could live. And the salary was higher.

The next day I went to my master's office. I was very nervous; I wanted so badly to leave. I asked him very politely, "Master?" "Humph?" he replied. "Master I wish to leave this house and find a new job for myself." "WHAT? Why would you want to do that? Have we mistreated you, have we not provided everything that is necessary for your survival?" he asked. "Yes master, but I would like to change my occupation as it has been five years of my service, and if it is alright with you, then I will take my leave sir." I said. "Have you found a job?" he asked. "No sir" I lied. "I am not allowed to leave the house." "So then how will you survive when you are looking for a job?" he asked. Marcos said: "There are times during the day when I have finished my work, and I could go out looking for a job then."

"If you can find another boy or girl who is as efficient as you then you will be allowed to leave from your service.  I will send one guard with you and give you two hours a day to look for someone to replace you, but once your two hours are up, you will return to this house and finish the rest of your chores. Do you understand?" he said in a very serious tone of voice." "Yes sir, as you wish." I left the room in a very happy mood.

For the next three weeks I looked for a replacement. During this time not any insult or beating could depress me. I was so happy. At last I found someone to take my place. Then I was free, and my new life was paradise. I had enough money to spend on things I wanted, and all of the food that I wanted for free. My room was a bit smaller but all the freedom that I enjoyed during my free time more than made up for the smaller living space. This was the life that I was waiting for. This is what I had worked for those five years.

Your assignment: In the text, find sentences that are important to the story because they are essential to the development of the plot.

**Here is what you might write.**

The sentence, "…hoping that one day I will have the freedom to go out when I want and to get a job outside of the house that I live and work in…" is important because it states the hope and dream of the main character Marcos, and most of the story is about Marcos's actions to make this hope and dream come true, as it finally does. The next two examples, "She and the master were always complaining about my work, and rarely complimented me, even though I tried to never disobey them." and "…I would get punished with beatings from the gardener," are important because they help the reader understand why Marcos wants to escape. "One night an idea struck me!" is important because it arouses interest in the reader to find out what the idea is, and leads into a description of the idea, which is the first step in Marcos's plan to escape.

The sentences, "For several weeks I struggled to find a proper job that would give me some time for myself, that also had a place for me to live, and paid a better salary. I finally found what I was looking for." are important because they tell what Marcos is doing to carry out his escape plan.

These two sentences, "The next day I went to my master's office." and "Master I wish to leave this house and find a new job for myself." tell about the next steps in his escape plan, the results of which he got the master to approve his job search and to lay out the Marcos obligation before leaving – to find his replacement.

In the last paragraph we read this: "At last I found someone to take my place. Then I was free, and my new life was paradise." It tells the reader that Marcos plan worked, he achieved his hope and dream.

Name: _____     Date: _____

You can scan the QR code given below or use the url to access additional EdSearch resources including videos and mobile apps related to *Develop Setting.*

  **Develop Setting**

| URL | QR Code |
| --- | --- |
| http://www.lumoslearning.com/a/rl65 |  |

The sky was dark and overcast. It had been raining all night long, and there was no sign of it stopping. I thought that my Sunday would be ruined. As it poured outside, I settled down by the window to watch the rain. The park opposite my house looked even more green and fresh than usual. The branches of the tall trees swayed so hard in the strong wind that I thought they would break. A few children were splashing about in the mud puddles and having a wonderful time. I wished I could join them too! There were very few people out on the road and those who were hurried on their way wrapped in raincoats and carrying umbrellas.

My mother announced that lunch was ready. It was piping hot and very welcoming in the damp weather. We spent the afternoon listening to music and to the downpour outside.

In the evening, we chatted and made paper boats that we meant to sail in the stream of water outside. It was not a bad day, after all!

**After reading the story, enter the details in the map below. This will help you answer the question with ease.**

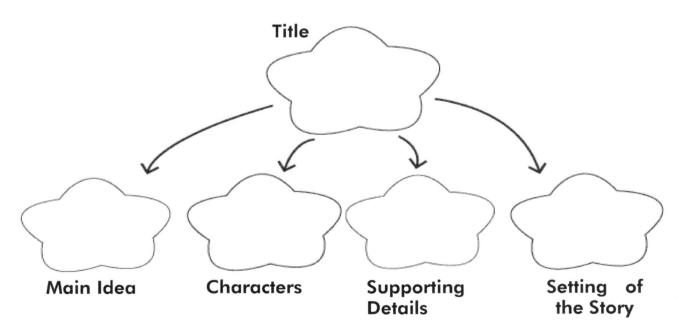

**Title**

**Main Idea**     **Characters**     **Supporting Details**     **Setting of the Story**

**1. What is the setting of the above story?**

Ⓐ   The home of the writer
Ⓑ   The park
Ⓒ   The writer's village
Ⓓ   The writer's office

One evening, long after most people had gone to bed, a friend and I were making our way merrily back home through the silent and almost deserted streets. We had been to a musical show and were talking about the actor we had seen and heard in it.

"That show made him a star overnight," said my friend about one of the actors. "He was completely unknown before, and now thousands of teenagers send him chocolates and love letters through the mail."

"I thought he was quite good," I said, "but not worth thousands of love letters daily. As a matter of fact, one of his songs gave me pain."

"Which was that?" my friend asked. "Sing to me." I burst into a parody of the song.

"Be quiet for heaven's sake!" My friend gave me an astonished look. "You'll give everybody a fright and wake people up for miles around."

"Never mind," I said, intoxicated with the sound of my own voice. "I don't care. How does it matter?"

And I went on singing the latest tunes at the top of my voice. Presently there came behind us the sound of heavy footsteps, and before you could say "Jack Robinson," a policeman was standing in front of me, his notebook open, and a determined look on his face.

"Excuse me, sir," he said. "You have a remarkable voice if I may say so. Who taught you to sing? I'd very much like to find someone who can give my daughter singing lessons. Would you be kind enough to tell me your name and address? Then my wife or I can drop you a line and discuss the matter."

**After reading the story, enter the details in the map below. This will help you answer the question with ease.**

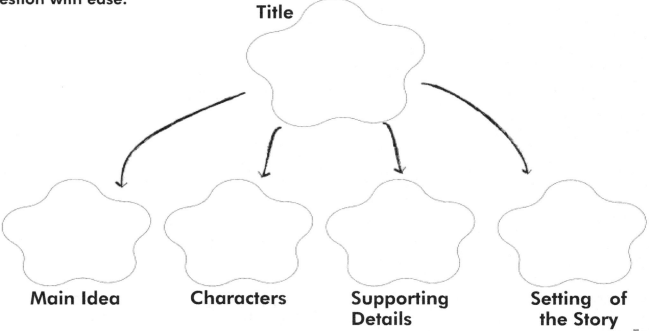

**2. What detail in the above story tells us that it took place late in the night?**

- Ⓐ  We had been to a musical show
- Ⓑ  "Be quiet for heaven's sake."
- Ⓒ  One evening, long after most people had gone to bed
- Ⓓ  And I went on singing the latest tunes at the top of my voice

Sally woke up earlier than she expected one morning. Something wasn't right. She then realized what had awakened her. It was an unfamiliar sound. She listened closely and realized that the sound was coming from outside. Climbing out of her bed, she slipped into her robe and slippers and went to the window. Looking out, she soon spotted a small kitten under the tree that stood outside her window. She stood, staring at the helpless creature. It didn't move. It soon spotted her and meowed, as if it were calling out to her.

Sally left her room and found her mother in the kitchen having her morning cup of coffee. She excitedly told her mom about the kitten. "I am going outside to get the poor little thing," she told her mother.

"I'll go with you," her mom replied. Together they walked into the backyard. The kitten was still there waiting for them. Sally picked it up in her arms. The little kitten felt so soft and cuddly in her arms. She had always wanted a kitten and wondered if her mother would allow her to keep him. Her mother decided to first feed the kitten. She also decided to make a few calls to see where he came from. The kitten certainly needed a home. Sally became more hopeful that she would be able to keep the kitten.

**After reading the story, enter the details in the map below. This will help you answer the questions with ease.**

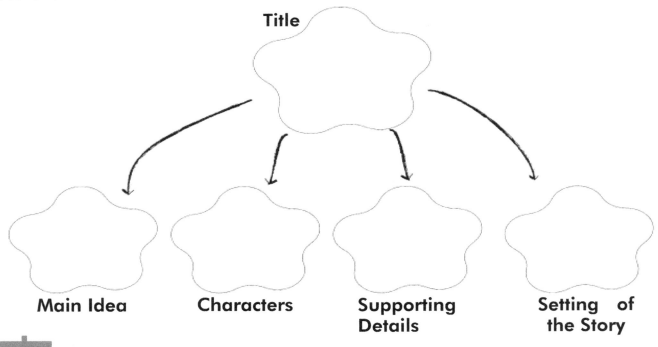

**3. What sentence(s) point(s) out the time of the story?**

Ⓐ Sally went out of her room and found her mother in the kitchen having her morning cup of coffee

Ⓑ Sally went out of her room and found her mother in the kitchen.

Ⓒ Sally woke up earlier than she expected one morning.

Ⓓ Both A and C

**4. From the story, we come to know that Sally lived _____.**

Ⓐ in a multi-storied building

Ⓑ in a downtown, urban area

Ⓒ in a motel

Ⓓ in a single family house with a backyard

The forest's sentinel
Glides silently across the hill
And perches in an old pine tree,
A friendly presence his!
No harm can come
From night bird on the prowl.
His cry is mellow,
Much softer than a peacock's call.

Why then this fear of owls
Calling in the night?
If men must speak,
Then owls must hoot-
They have the right.
On me it casts no spell:
Rather, it seems to cry,
The night is good- all's well, all's well."

- RUSKIN BOND

**5. The setting of this poem is in a _____.**

Ⓐ Sports stadium

Ⓑ Forest

Ⓒ House

Ⓓ Palace

**6. What is the setting of a story?**

Ⓐ Who and where the story takes place
Ⓑ When and where the story takes place
Ⓒ When and why the story takes place
Ⓓ How and where the story takes place

Ralphie lived in the oldest and largest house on the block. Ralphie's friends were scared to visit him because of how worn down his house looked. The outside of the house was gray with cracks in the stucco and lots of spider webs hanging off it.

**7. What is the setting of the story?**

Ⓐ Inside Ralphie's house
Ⓑ Inside Ralphie's friends' houses
Ⓒ Outside Ralphie's house
Ⓓ None of the above

The thieves intended to rob the bank around dinner time. They figured most people would be home eating with their families, so it would be easy for them to get in and out of the big green and gold bank.

**8. What is the setting of the story?**

Ⓐ The bank on Green Street
Ⓑ The bank on Green Street at 7 pm
Ⓒ The green and gold bank at dinner time
Ⓓ The green and gold bank in the morning

Janice had her last final exam of the year; she was very excited and wanted to celebrate. After the final, she would no longer be a high school student.

**9. In what month was it most likely this last exam occurred?**

Ⓐ In April
Ⓑ In June
Ⓒ In September
Ⓓ In December

Noah was excited that he got to share his birthday with his aunt. They were both born on the same day, just nineteen years apart. Their birthday was on April 13th.

**10. In what season is Noah's birthday? Circle the correct answer**

- Ⓐ  In the spring
- Ⓑ  In the summer
- Ⓒ  In the winter
- Ⓓ  In the fall

Tom looked out his window as he spoke on the phone with his mother. He told her about his day and the new job he just was offered. When Tom talked on the phone, he often looked out the window and would see Thomas Jefferson's monument. It was amazing that he lived in a city with so many beautiful, historical monuments, the White House and the U.S. Capitol.

**11. Where does Tom live?**

- Ⓐ  New York City
- Ⓑ  Washington State
- Ⓒ  Delaware
- Ⓓ  Washington, D.C.

# The Road Not Taken, By Robert Frost

Two roads diverged in a yellow wood,
And sorry I could not travel both
And be one traveler, long I stood
And looked down one as far as I could
To where it bent in the undergrowth;

Then took the other, as just as fair,
And having perhaps the better claim,
Because it was grassy and wanted wear;
Though as for that the passing there
Had worn them really about the same,

And both that morning equally lay
In leaves no step had trodden black.
Oh, I kept the first for another day!
Yet knowing how way leads on to way,
I doubted if I should ever come back.

I shall be telling this with a sigh
Somewhere ages and ages hence:
Two roads diverged in a wood, and
I took the one less traveled by,
And that has made all the difference.

**12. Find the rhyming pattern and describe it. Write your answer in the box below.**

# Chapter 2

## Lesson 10: Author's Purpose in a Text

*Before answering the questions, it is important to understand the meaning of different points of view.*

**Author's Point of View**

As an author, you need to decide from which point of view you are writing to the reader: first person, second person or third person. Also, if you are reading a work written by some other author, you should be able to understand how your opinion differs from what the author is saying or writing about.

**First person:** The author is the one telling the story to the reader. The story may be about a topic the author has actually experienced or seen (nonfiction), or a topic that the author made-up (fiction). When writing in the first person, the author does not give directions or instructions to the reader. Also, the author uses the personal pronouns I, we, me, us, my, mine, our or ours in the essay.

**Second person:** The author is addressing the reader, giving instructions or suggestions for the reader to follow. The author will use the personal pronouns you or yours in the essay.

**Third person:** The author is not a character in the story, but is a narrator telling the story as an outside observer. The narrator may or may not know all the thoughts and feelings of one or more characters in the story. The author will use the personal pronouns he, she, it, him, his, her, hers, it or its in the essay.

**You can scan the QR code given below or use the url to access additional EdSearch resources including videos and mobile apps related to *Author's Purpose in a Text*.**

## Author's Purpose in a Text

| URL | QR Code |
|-----|---------|
| http://www.lumoslearning.com/a/rl66 |  |

In the original version of the story "The Three Little Pigs," the wolf chases the pigs and say he will huff and puff and blow their houses down.

**The following paragraph is a different interpretation.**

I've always been misunderstood. I'm allergic to hay. I can't help it that when I'm near hay, I huff an I puff and I sometimes blow things down. No one has any reason to be afraid of me, but sometime they are. What happened to those poor little pigs is sad, but it was their own fault.

**1. Who is talking in this paragraph?** _____

_____

**2. How is the narrator's point of view different from the traditional one?**

 Ⓐ He claims that he had no intention of blowing down the pigs' houses or of eating them, bu that his allergies were at fault.

 Ⓑ He claims that he had no intention of blowing down the pigs' house, but wanted to eat ther up.

 Ⓒ He claims that he had no intention of blowing down the pigs' houses or of eating them, bu he just wanted to scare them.

 Ⓓ He claims that another wolf blew the pigs' houses down and blamed it on him.

**3. Why does the narrator claim to have been misunderstood?**

 Ⓐ Because everyone has regarded him as a bully who wants to occupy weaker animals' house

 Ⓑ Because everyone has regarded him as a pig-killing villain when he had no such intention.

 Ⓒ Because everyone has regarded him sick and allergy-ridden.

 Ⓓ Because he is evil.

I was shaking like a leaf. My palms were sweaty and I was so nervous about my presentation.

**4. What point of view is this from?**

 Ⓐ Third person omniscient

 Ⓑ Second person

 Ⓒ First person

 Ⓓ Third person

Name: _____          Date: _____

Heather loved her new dog. She played with it every day and took it for walks. The dog became Heather's best friend, and they did everything together.

**5. What point of view is this told in?**

Ⓐ First person
Ⓑ Second person
Ⓒ Third person
Ⓓ None of the above

**In the original version of "Little Red Riding Hood," Red is delivering food to her sick grand-mother when she stumbles upon a wolf in the house.**

**The following is a different interpretation of "Little Red Riding Hood,"**

I'd been after that wolf for a long time, but when I went into the woods that day to deliver a basket to my grandmother, I promised my mother that I wouldn't leave the path to go wolf-hunting, even if I got a clear shot. I even spoke politely to him and did exactly as my mother asked. But when I got to grandma's house, I found that he had eaten her! I was determined to get revenge. Thank goodness the woodcutter came along and did my job for me. I don't need to get into any trouble with my mother, but it really burns me up when people think I couldn't have handled the wolf by myself!

**6. Who is talking in this passage?**

Ⓐ Red Riding Hood in the story "Little Red Riding Hood"
Ⓑ The wolf in the story "Little Red Riding Hood"
Ⓒ The mother in the story "Little Red Riding Hood"
Ⓓ A narrator

**7. How is the narrator's point of view different from the traditional one?**

Ⓐ She is traditionally thought of as a brave girl who wanted to fight the wily wolf.
Ⓑ The narrator's point of view is not different from the traditional one.
Ⓒ She is traditionally thought of as an innocent child, in danger from the wily wolf.
Ⓓ She is thought of as a mean girl who hates wolfs.

**8. Why does the narrator claim to have been misunderstood?**

Ⓐ She wanted people to think that she is a brave girl.
Ⓑ People think she couldn't have defeated the wolf.
Ⓒ People think that she does not follow her mother's instructions.
Ⓓ Both A and B

The forest's sentinel
Glides silently across the hill
And perches in an old pine tree,
A friendly presence his!
No harm can come
From night bird on the prowl.
His cry is mellow,
Much softer than a peacock's call.

Why then this fear of owls
Calling in the night?
If men must speak,
Then owls must hoot-
They have the right.
On me it casts no spell:
Rather, it seems to cry,
"The night is good- all's well, all's well."

-- RUSKIN BOND

**9. In the above poem the author says 'If men must speak, Then owls must hoot-They have the right.' What does he mean by this?**

Ⓐ   That people should hoot like owls.
Ⓑ   That owls should talk like people.
Ⓒ   That owls hoot for the same reasons people speak. This is the way owls communicate.
Ⓓ   That owls do not have the right to talk.

**10. Which of the following are usually written in the second person point of view?**

Ⓐ   Instructions
Ⓑ   Self-help books
Ⓒ   Directions
Ⓓ   All of the above

**11. What does the poet say in regards to the two roads?**
   **Choose all that apply.**

Ⓐ   One of the roads is less traveled.
Ⓑ   He chose the one less traveled.
Ⓒ   He might try the first road another day, but doubts he will return.
Ⓓ   He doesn't like the looks of the railroad.

## Chapter 2

## Lesson 11: Compare Author's Writing to Another

*Let us understand the concept with an example.*

### Amelia Earhart, Aviatrix (female aviator)[1]

Amelia Mary Earhart was a famous American aviation pioneer. Some of her achievements: woman's world altitude record: 14,000 feet (1922), first woman to fly across the Atlantic solo (1932), first woman to fly nonstop, coast-to-coast across the U.S. (1933), first person to fly solo nonstop from Mexico City, Mexico to Newark, New Jersey (1935).

Aviation, especially piloting aircraft, was a male dominated career. Her choice to enter it was not unusual for her; throughout her childhood, she aspired to a future career and kept a scrapbook of newspaper clippings about successful women in predominantly male-oriented fields. And piloting aircraft was one of those fields.

But she did not enter the field of aviation right away. During Christmas vacation in 1917, Earhart visited her sister in Toronto. World War I had been raging and Earhart saw the returning wounded soldiers. After receiving training as a nurse's aide from the Red Cross, she began work with the Voluntary Aid Detachment at Spadina Military Hospital in Toronto. When the 1918 Spanish flu pandemic reached Toronto, Earhart was engaged in arduous nursing duties that included night shifts at the Spadina Military Hospital.

At about that time, Earhart and a friend visited an air fair in Toronto. One of the highlights of the day was a flying exhibition put on by a World War I ace. The pilot overhead spotted Earhart and her friend, who were watching from an isolated clearing, and dived at them. "I did not understand it at the time," she said, "but I believe that little red airplane said something to me as it swished by." She quit the hospital job a year later to be with her parents in California.

In Long Beach, on December 28, 1920, Earhart and her father visited an airfield where Frank Hawks (who later gained fame as an air racer) gave her a ride that would forever change Earhart's life. "By the time I had got two or three hundred feet off the ground," she said, "I knew I had to fly." After that 10-minute flight she immediately became determined to learn to fly. Working at a variety of jobs, she managed to save $1,000 for flying lessons, and began her aviation career.

Early in 1936, Earhart started to plan a round-the-world flight. Not the first to circle the globe, it would be the longest at 29,000 miles, following a grueling equatorial route. With financing from Purdue University, in July 1936, a Lockheed Electra 10E was built at Lockheed Aircraft Company to

her specifications, which included extensive modifications to the fuselage to incorporate a large fu
tank. During the attempt to make a circumnavigation of the globe in 1937 in this aircraft, Earhart, he
navigator and the aircraft disappeared over the central Pacific Ocean near Howland Island. Althoug
there was an extensive search for them, they were never found.

[1] Wikipedia contributors. "Amelia Earhart." Wikipedia, The Free Encyclopedia. Wikipedia, The Fre
Encyclopedia, 24 Aug. 2017. Web. 27 Aug. 2017

## The Road Not Taken [2]
By Robert Frost

Two roads diverged in a yellow wood,
And sorry I could not travel both
And be one traveler, long I stood
And looked down one as far as I could
To where it bent in the undergrowth;
Then took the other, as just as fair,
And having perhaps the better claim,
Because it was grassy and wanted wear;
Though as for that the passing there
Had worn them really about the same,
And both that morning equally lay
In leaves no step had trodden black.
Oh, I kept the first for another day!
Yet knowing how way leads on to way,
I doubted if I should ever come back.
I shall be telling this with a sigh
Somewhere ages and ages hence:
Two roads diverged in a wood, and I—
I took the one less traveled by,
And that has made all the difference.

[2] Robert Frost, Stopping by Woods on a Snowy Evening, from The Poetry of Robert Frost, edited by
Edward Connery Lathem. Copyright 1923, © 1969 by Henry Holt and Company, Inc. renewed 195
by Robert Frost. Reprinted with the permission of Henry Holt and Company, LLC.

**To meet the requirements of the standard, this is what you might write.**

What could the career of the famous aviatrix Amelia Earhart and a verse from a poem by poet Robe
Frost have in common? They both "…took the one (road) less traveled by, And that has made all th
difference." From the poem, I inferred that at some point in his life, Frost was faced with a difficu
career choice (a choice between being a poet and being something else) and that looking backward
at that choice, expresses satisfaction with the choice he made, saying "I took the one less traveled b
And that has made all the difference." Presumably, if he had made the other career choice, he wou

not have written the poem and we would not have had the chance to enjoy it.

If Amelia Earhart had not been exposed to the flying exhibition at the air fair, had not given up her nursing job at the hospital to join her parents in California, and had not been taken for an airplane ride by Frank Hawks, then chances are she would have remained in Toronto at the hospital working as a nurse. She would not have become famous breaking flight records, or encouraging women to become pilots, or making other contributions to companies and agencies in the field of aviation.

And so you can see that the poet communicated his choice by producing poetry; the aviatrix communicated her choice by participating in aviation, her field of choice, as an aviatrix, an author and a member of organizations in the aviation industry.

Publisher's note: There are critics and the poet himself who contend the poem was not about expressing satisfaction about a choice the poet made, but rather a comment on people who make one choice and then worry about not making the other choice.

**You can scan the QR code given below or use the url to access additional EdSearch resources including videos and mobile apps related to *Compare Author's Writing to Another.***

| ed)Search | *Compare Author's Writing to Another* |
|---|---|
| **URL** | **QR Code** |
| http://www.lumoslearning.com/a/rl69 | |

If your actions inspire others to dream more, learn more, do more and become more, you are a leader. - John Quincy Adams

The key to successful leadership today is influence, not authority.- Kenneth Blanchard

**1. Pick the right statement that brings out the meaning of the above quotations.**

Ⓐ  Adams talks about actions, whereas Blanchard talks of authority.
Ⓑ  Adams talks about leadership by inspiration, whereas Blanchard talks of leadership by influence.
Ⓒ  Adams talks about inspiration, whereas Blanchard talks of influence.
Ⓓ  Adams talks about leadership, whereas Blanchard talks of success.

**Read the following passage and answer the questions that follows.**

The square is probably the best known of the quadrilaterals. It is defined as having all sides equal. All its interior angles are right angles (90°). From this it follows that the opposite sides are also parallel. A square is simply a specific case of a regular polygon, in this case with 4 sides. All the facts and properties described for regular polygons apply to a square.

The rectangle, like the square, is one of the most commonly known quadrilaterals. It is defined as having all four interior angles 90° (right angles). The opposite sides of a rectangle are parallel and congruent.

**2. A similarity between a square and rectangle is that _____.**

Ⓐ  all the sides are equal in both the figures
Ⓑ  only opposite sides are equal in both the figures
Ⓒ  all the interior angles are right angles
Ⓓ  none of the angles are right angles

**3. Fill in the Blank**

**A difference between a square and rectangle is that _____.**

**Read the statements carefully and answer the questions that follow.**

1. Teachers who inspire know that teaching is like cultivating a garden, and those who would have nothing to do with thorns must never attempt to gather flowers.
~Author Unknown

2. Teachers who inspire realize that there will always be rocks in the road ahead of us. They will be stumbling blocks or stepping stones; it all depends on how we use them.
~Author Unknown

4. **While the first author says that teaching is like cultivating a garden, the second author says that _____.**

Ⓐ those teachers who would have nothing to do with thorns must never attempt to gather flowers
Ⓑ inspiring teachers realize that there will be rocks in the road ahead
Ⓒ inspiring teachers realize that there will only be stepping stones in the road
Ⓓ inspiring teachers realize that there will be only flowers and no thorns

5. **Both the quotations are about _____.**

Ⓐ stumbling blocks
Ⓑ rocks and stepping stones
Ⓒ gardens, flowers and thorns
Ⓓ teachers who inspire

6. **Hurricanes are similar to blizzards because _____.**

Ⓐ They both are rain storms.
Ⓑ They both cause heavy destruction.
Ⓒ They both are man-made storms.
Ⓓ They both involve snow.

7. **Love is _____ to a roller coaster because there are many twists and turns in both.**

Ⓐ different
Ⓑ unequal
Ⓒ similar
Ⓓ All of the above

When you wash dishes you want to make sure you use soap to scrub the dirt off and make sure yo rinse them clean after.

**8. Which of the tasks below are similar to washing dishes?**

Ⓐ Cleaning your house
Ⓑ Washing the laundry
Ⓒ Folding your clothes
Ⓓ Cooking dinner

**9. Words that are used to compare things are _____.**

Ⓐ Like
Ⓑ Same as
Ⓒ Both A and B
Ⓓ In Contrast

**10. A word that is used to contrast two things is _____.**

Ⓐ Too
Ⓑ However
Ⓒ More
Ⓓ And

# End of Reading: Literature

# Answer Key and
# Detailed Explanations

## Chapter 2: Reading: Literature

# Lesson 1: Analysis of Key Events and Ideas

| Question No. | Answer | Detailed Explanations |
|---|---|---|
| 1 | B | The author used very descriptive language to pull the reader in. The author wants the reader to be able to imagine what the moment is like. It was raining and the wind was blowing, but the author's point was for the reader to be able to picture it. |
| 2 | B | Although the author is talking about the night owl, the point of view is actually that of the author. |
| 3 | A | The poem mentions that it's a night bird and, at the end, again mentions night. The answer is A. |
| 4 Part A | A | Answer A is correct. Upon reading the passage, you will see in the second paragraph that it directly says that they found the bones of a lion. |
| 4 Part B | A | If you chose A, you read the passage correctly. The last sentence in the first paragraph gives the correct answer. |
| 5 | C | If you chose answer C, you got it right. Good Sense told the other men NOT to create the lion. |
| 6 | C | Answer C is the correct answer because it's a direct quote in the story that the friend was afraid the singing would disturb others. The policeman was not behind them yet, or at least had not been noticed. There was no mention of the friend being embarrassed. |
| 7 | C | The only answer choice that shows a desire to play outside is C. |
| 8 | C | Answer choice C is correct. The fact that it goes by stations tells you that you're on a train. |
| 9 | Ring | Ring. This is given in the very first paragraph of the passage. |

# Lesson 2: Conclusions Drawn from the Text

| Question No. | Answer | Detailed Explanations |
|---|---|---|
| 1 | A | The correct answer is A. Sarah's mother told her that it was going to rain, but Sarah chose to ignore her mother's advice. None of the other answers are true. There is no evidence that she doesn't love her mother, and if she didn't like getting wet then she would have definitely listened to her mother. She did not obey her mother, so answer choice D is not correct. |
| 2 | C | The correct answer is C. Sarah would not have argued about whether or not to take an umbrella if it were raining. She would not need an umbrella if it were snowing or if it were warm. |
| 3 | B | The correct answer is B. We can tell that it is a negative emotion that the boy is feeling - so that eliminates A and D. If he were scared, he would likely want to be WITH people, not away from them. |
| 4 | C | The correct answer is C. All of the foods mentioned were breakfast foods, so you can assume that breakfast is being cooked. Also, coffee is usually brewed first thing in the morning. |
| 5 | D | In this day and age, it is not likely that the store owner would let him pay him later or work off the candy. John would have to go home and get the money and walk back to the store. |
| 6 | D | D is the correct answer. The story specifically says that he did not like books and that he was very clever. Nothing was said in the story that he did not like the other boys. |
| 7 | C | The correct answer is C. If the article is saying that these people need to be active, then we can assume that they normally do a lot of sitting. |
| 8 | D | The answer is D. The passage specifically says that it was raining and there was no sign of it stopping. The passage does not mention wintry weather or sunny day. |
| 9 | C | The answer is C. The fact that the officers called him sir is the only detail that shows that it is a male. |
| 10 | C | The correct answer is C. The dog hid under the table AFTER the loud noise, so we can assume that the dog was scared by the loud noises associated with the thunderstorm. |
| 11 | Fall | Pumpkins are associated with fall and Halloween, and that is the only season where the leaves change color. |
| 12 | C | The author is proud of his/her dog and is saying that the dog can learn tricks and therefore, the dog is really smart. |
| 13 | D | Every statement supports the idea that the writer misses Jamie. |

# Lesson 3: Development of Ideas

| Question No. | Answer | Detailed Explanations |
|---|---|---|
| 1 | D | The correct answer is D because it is a good ending sentence and sums up the point of the paragraph. A and B are too specific, and C is repetitive. |
| 2 | A | The only answer that is a concluding sentence is answer choice A. It mentions class president, which is the point of the article. The other three answers are specific details and do not sum up the passage. |
| 3 | D | Answer choice D is correct. It correctly summarizes the point of the article. The other three answers do not make sense if you read the passage carefully. |
| 4 | A | The correct answer is A. Loving the smell of sea water supports loving the beach as far as a vacation trip. Although there are starfish in the ocean and sometimes aircraft fly by, neither of those details support the main idea of the paragraph. The author would not like vacationing at the beach if he/she hated the smell of sea water, so B is not correct. |
| 5 | D | Answer choice D is correct. All of the statements about Christmas are positive, so this detail will be positive too. All of the other answer choices are negative. |
| 6 | B | While all of the titles make sense, the best title would be B, "A Pleasant Surprise." The character in the story was very pleasantly surprised that he was not in trouble with the policeman. |
| 7 | A | The correct answer is A. Although all of the answers are true statements, the only one that gives the detail of the sky being cloudy is saying it is "dark and overcast." |
| 8 | A | The correct answer is A. The mothers specifically told the girls to stay together and stay away from strangers. Answer choices B and C are opposite of what the mothers told their daughters. |
| 9 | A | Answer A is the correct choice. The primary message of the passage is that it is rewarding to help others. Although giving people food helps them not to go hungry, it is only one detail of the passage. There is no evidence to show receiving the items changes people's lives, and helping others does not always mean giving blankets. |
| 10 | C | The correct answer is C. Allison worked very hard and did not give up, and she eventually accomplished her goal. A is not correct because it will take people different amounts of time to accomplish what they set out to do. The key is to never give up. D is the opposite of what the passage is saying, and B is never mentioned. |

Name: _____  Date: _____

| Question No. | Answer | Detailed Explanations |
|---|---|---|
| 11 | preservative | preservative. This is given in the very first paragraph of the passage. |
| 12 | | |

Dear Mayor,

I know you are very busy, but there is an important issue I would like to address with you. The park in my neighborhood doesn't have enough tennis courts to accommodate all of the people who want to use them. Almost everyone in my neighborhood enjoys playing tennis, but there is only one court for all of us to share. This is a problem for many reasons.

First, most of us have to wait for hours to play tennis because there is only one court. This is inconvenient because we all try to come and play after school, and instead of getting to have some fun after school, we are waiting for hours to play one game. Tennis is a great way to keep kids active instead of them sitting on a couch and playing video games. Adding additional courts will help solve both these problems and keep the kids in your town active and healthy.

Next, the younger kids who want to play often have to go home before they even have the opportunity to get one game in. The parents enjoy knowing their kids are at the tennis courts and do not worry about them. However, if they continue having to wait so long, they may get bored and do something else, which may get them in trouble. Having a safe place for the kids to go is important.

I know that the budget is tight this year, but I think that an additional tennis court would be a good investment for the neighborhood. Tennis is a great sport to play with friends and family. It helps keep us out of trouble by giving us something positive to do with our time. It helps keep us in shape and helps us learn friendly competition. When we play doubles, it also helps us learn to work in teams.

If you are not able to add another tennis court at our park, I hope you will at least consider it. It would be good for our whole community.

Sincerely,
Tommy Brown
Grade 6

# Lesson 4: Summary of Text

| Question No. | Answer | Detailed Explanations |
|---|---|---|
| 1 | B | Answer choice B is correct because the story specifically says that the policeman asked the writer for his name and address. You assume that the man gave it to him. |
| 2 | | By reading this you can conclude that Thomas likes sports. Based on the fact that Thomas plays so many sports and likes to run in his free time, we can conclude that he likes sports. |
| 3 | D | Because he is being so careful, you know that ladders can be dangerous. The correct answer is D. Age is never mentioned, neither is ladders being easy or fun. |
| 4 | A | The correct answer is A. The paragraph mentions nothing about students who enjoy math and it doesn't mention how many to buy. It also does not say anything about not needing all of the items. |
| 5 | A | The passage is positive about younger siblings, so the answer choice will be positive. It is obvious that the author of the passage thinks that having younger siblings is great. |
| 6 | A | The correct answer is A. Because he spent all of the 5 dollars at the candy store, you can assume that he loves candy and did not think spending the money would be useless. That is the only answer that could be right. It never mentions what color his piggy bank is or sharing his candy. |
| 7 | B | The correct answer is B. It does not mention whether or not she has had her own room before or not. Her mother is not even mentioned and it said she was decorating her room pink, not purple. |
| 8 | B | The correct answer is B. The passage does not mention what state he is moving to, and it also does not mention that he didn't want to stop in other states along the way. |
| 9 | C | Answer choice C is correct because the poem has a sad mood. The girl is feeling sad and unhappy. It does not mention that she is afraid and we know that she is not excited. Even though she went to her room, it does not mention that she wanted to be alone. |
| 10 | A | Based on the passage, the boy was moving to start a new life. They did not say that he was going on vacation, trying to make it as an actor, or looking for his brother. That's why we can assume that he is starting a new life. |

| Question No. | Answer | Detailed Explanations |
|---|---|---|
| 11 Part A | B | The story was not only about a man named Good Sense, it was about having good sense and using good judgment. The three men acted before they thought, and should have listened to Good Sense. |
| 11 Part B | D | Answer choice D is correct because the three friends should have listened to Good Sense's advice and they should have also thought through the consequences before they acted, as described in answers A and C. Answer B is not correct because while Good Sense does not like to read, he is still clever and avoided being eaten by the lion. |
| 12 | A | Option A is the correct answer.

Poet's purpose is stated throughout the small poem. |

# Lesson 5: Characters Responses and Changes

| Question No. | Answer | Detailed Explanations |
|---|---|---|
| 1 | D | Answer choice D is correct. There are only three characters in the story; the writer, the writer's friend, and the policeman. Although the actor is mentioned, he is not an actual character. |
| 2 | C | The correct answer is C. They were talking about the man in the musical show they had just seen. |
| 3 | C | The correct answer is C. The writer is writing in 1st person, and she is the main character in her story. |
| 4 | B | The correct answer is B. A major character will be a major part of the story. They will be in more of the story than minor characters. |
| 5 | D | The answer is D, all of the above. If you missed this question, go back and re-read the story. Each of these characters contributed action to the story. |
| 6 | A | The correct answer is A. The protagonist is often the good guy in a story. He/she is the main character of the story. |
| 7 | C | Character traits are the descriptions that authors give their characters. The answer is C. |
| 8 | A | Jane was very positive about starting a new school, so we are looking for a positive answer. They are all negative emotions except easy-going. |
| 9 | D | The answer choice is D. Risking his own life to save a dog's life shows the man thinks of others more than himself. |
| 10 | C | Greg was trying to see how things worked, not being mean to people. The answer choice is C. He was curious. |
| 11 | | The answer should include that the magician wanted Aladdin to give him the lamp, but Aladdin could not at the time. |
| 12 | | 1. Alma mater - graduated from<br>2. Pas de deaux - dance step with 2 people<br>3. Carte blanche - full discretionary power<br>4, Bon appetite - salutation to eat<br>5. Tete a tete - a private meeting between 2 people<br>6. Quid pro quo - contract made between parties for services<br>7. Alfresco - outside<br>8. Caveat emptor - buyer beware |

# Lesson 6: Figurative Words and Phrases

| Question No. | Answer | Detailed Explanations |
|---|---|---|
| 1 | A | The answer is A. "dead to the world" means that he was asleep. He would not stay at home if he was not breathing or unconscious; he would be removed immediately and his family would be upset. |
| 2 | A | Being in hot water means being in trouble, so answer choice A is correct. |
| 3 | A | The correct answer is A. There is no such thing as a circular file, so the only possibility is the trashcan. To say that means to throw something away. |
| 4 | B | Working like a dog means working really hard, so answer choice B is correct. This is a common saying. |
| 5 | A | Mules are known to be stubborn, so answer choice A is correct. |
| 6 | B | A mountain of work is a lot of work. Answer choice B is correct. |
| 7 | C | A train wreck causes a big mess on the tracks. Answer choice C is correct. |
| 8 | D | Being a star doesn't mean you have to be famous. When you are really good at something, you are said to be "a star". Answer choice D is correct. |
| 9 | D | Being a rock means that you are there for someone to lean on. Answer choice D is correct. |
| 10 | D | When someone says they feel like a million bucks, it means they feel great. The correct answer is D. Elated means the same thing as happy. Discontented means the opposite. |
| 11 | D | Putting your foot in your mouth means you said something you wish you could take back. |
| 12 | A | Bugging someone and bothering someone are the same thing, so the correct answer is A. |
| 13 | C | Quitting something cold turkey means that you quit suddenly and do it alone without any help. |

# Lesson 7: Connotative Words and Phrases

| Question No. | Answer | Detailed Explanations |
| --- | --- | --- |
| 1 | A | Thrifty means that you don't want to spend money unless you have to and you want to save as much as possible. Answer choice A is correct. |
| 2 | B | Because the author of this sentence admitted that he/she didn't like the trait, we know there is a negative spin on the part of the author. That's why the correct answer is B. |
| 3 | C | 'Courageous' is the word with the positive connotation. |
| 4 | D | Brambles are prickly bushes or shrubs. It specifically says that he was "all by himself" so we know other people weren't around. |
| 5 | C | It was very nice for the girl to ask the new student to join in. C is the answer. |
| 6 | B | Because they are characterized as being "sweet and polite" we would assume their actions would be in line with that. Answer choices A and D are very rude and hateful. Answer choice B is more of the way a sweet and polite couple would react. |
| 7 | A | The fact that they had to keep looking for supplies tells us that there were not enough supplies. The correct answer is A. |
| 8 | C | Affect is the correct word for the verb in this sentence. |
| 9 | C | The positive connotation of the words in the sentence show us that the candidate won. That is why C is the correct answer |
| 10 | B | The answer is B. Tragic is the only negative word that works in this sentence. |
| 11 | B | The girl obviously has no respect for anyone or anything. She would be classified a brat for sure. B is the correct answer. |

# Lesson 8: Meaning of Words and Phrases

| Question No. | Answer | Detailed Explanations |
|---|---|---|
| 1 | B | Answer choice B is correct. Based on the sentences, it is clear that the person being discussed has come to fame recently. |
| 2 | A | The first part of the poem is how the owl comes out of the tree into the forest at night. The correct answer is A. |
| 3 | D | The poet said all of the above things in the opening lines of the poem. |
| 4 | A | The author did not seem excited, but was definitely not negative (annoyed or sad.) The correct answer is A. |
| 5 | A | Because the man had helped the lion, the man's life was spared. Even though it is a human and an animal, it is a story of friendship. The correct answer is A. |
| 6 | A | The correct answer is A. The teacher asked the student to share the story so that maybe more kids would wear helmets. |
| 7 | A | Ominous is kind of creepy and spooky. That is definitely the mood here. The answer is A. |
| 8 | B | When you hear that statement, it makes you feel badly for that man. The answer choice that is correct is B. |
| 9 | C | Answer choice C is correct. Even though the brother isn't always nice to his sister, his actions show her that he loves her. |
| 10 | D | Answer choice D is correct based on the poem. The author talks about moving forward and forgetting. |
| 11 | C | Based on the sentences, it is obvious that Joe likes to make people laugh. |
| 12 | A | Answer choice A shows us the lesson in the passage. |

# Lesson 9: Develop Setting

| Question No. | Answer | Detailed Explanations |
|---|---|---|
| 1 | A | Based on the details in the passage, it is obvious that the writer is a child still living at home. They discuss doing things that would take place in a home. For those reasons, the correct answer is A. |
| 2 | C | The story specifically says that it took place long after people had gone to bed, so answer choice C is correct. |
| 3 | D | The correct answer is D. The story specifically says it is morning and she found her mother in the kitchen drinking coffee. |
| 4 | D | The correct answer is D. It couldn't be a motel because her mother was in the kitchen sipping coffee. The backyard indicates they are not in an urban area. The most logical answer is that they live in just a regular single family home. |
| 5 | B | The answer is B, a forest. The poem never mentions a sports stadium, a house or a palace, but it mentions the forest in the opening line. |
| 6 | B | The answer is B. The setting of a story is when and where a story takes place |
| 7 | C | The answer is C. The only place mentioned is the outside of Ralphie's house, so that is the only option. |
| 8 | C | The correct answer is C. The story specifically says that the robbery was going to take place during dinner time and it was going to be at the green and gold bank |
| 9 | B | Because it's her last final exam of high school, you know that the setting of the story is in June. |
| 10 | A | The correct answer is A. The month of April is definitely in the spring. |
| 11 | D | All of the things mentioned are in Washington, D.C., our nation's capital. |
| 12 | | First, third, fourth rhyme, then second and fifth rhyme.<br><br>In the first paragraph, wood, stood and could rhyme while both and undergrowth rhyme.<br><br>In paragraph, fair, wear, there rhyme whereas claim and same rhyme.<br><br>Similarly, this pattern can be seen in all the paragraphs. Hence, First, third, fourth rhyme, then second and fifth rhyme. |

# Lesson 10: Author's Purpose in a Text

| Question No. | Answer | Detailed Explanations |
| --- | --- | --- |
| 1 | | Based on what he says, you can tell that these words are from the wolf's perspective. |
| 2 | A | In the above passage the wolf claims that allergies were to blame and he didn't want to hurt the pigs. That is very different from the traditional story. |
| 3 | B | He is trying to act innocent by saying he never meant to hurt the pigs. |
| 4 | C | Because "I" is used, we know that it is written from first person point of view. |
| 5 | C | The story does not use I or you; therefore, it is written in third person. |
| 6 | A | This passage was definitely from Little Red Riding Hood's perspective. The mother is never mentioned, but the wolf is. Therefore, it can't be from his perspective. |
| 7 | C | Answer choice C is correct. She is very sweet and innocent in the original story. She believes things that most of us wouldn't. |
| 8 | D | She wanted people to think she could have handled herself just fine against the wolf and that she wasn't scared at all. |
| 9 | C | Answer choice C is correct. The author clearly says that owls have the right to hoot if men have the right to speak. |
| 10 | D | Anytime someone is giving instructions or telling you what to do, it will be written in second person. D is the correct answer. |
| 11 | A,B & C | Options A,B,C are the correct answers.<br><br>These are all examples of the poet's purpose in the poem. The last D is not found. |

# Lesson 11: Compare Author's Writing to Another

| Question No. | Answer | Detailed Explanations |
|---|---|---|
| 1 | B | Answer choice B is correct. They are both talking about what types of leadership are best. They weren't just talking about inspiration and influence, but they were talking about leadership by inspiration and influence. |
| 2 | C | Based on the passage, we know that in both figures all of the angles are 90 degree angles (right angles). The correct answer is C. |
| 3 | | Based on the passage, we know that a square is defined as having all sides equal whereas the opposite sides of a rectangle are parallel and congruent. |
| 4 | B | Answer choice B is correct. Upon careful reading of the passage, you will see that the author specifically says that there will be rocks in the road ahead. The author does not say the rocks will always be stepping stones; some will be stumbling. |
| 5 | D | Both passages use metaphors to describe inspirational teachers, with the rocks and thorns being symbols for obstacles in their way. The correct answer is D. |
| 6 | B | The only answer statement that is true is B. A hurricane involves rain and a snowstorm involves snow but both storms can cause heavy destruction. |
| 7 | C | Similar is the same as "like." That is why the answer is C. |
| 8 | B | Answer choice B is the most similar because you use soap and water and have to rinse and dry them. |
| 9 | C | Like and Same as are both words we use to compare things. Contrast is a word we use to tell how things are different. The answer is C. |
| 10 | B | "However" is the only word that is a word you could use to contrast something. It is similar to the word "but." |

| Question No. | Answer | Detailed Explanations |
|---|---|---|
| 11 | | Huckleberry Finn : by Keith Neilson in which he discusses Huckleberry Finn's dilemma over, turning in a runaway slave that he believes to be the legal property of his owners. Given opportunities to turn Jim in, Huck finds that he cannot; his feelings toward Jim have become too strong. Huck begins to experience emotions that he has never had before & personal concern, loyalty, guilt, and fear. He is soon forced to accept Jim, not as a slave, but as a human being, and once he does that, all the contradictions of his moral situation become evident to the reader, if not immediately to Huck. He is forced to consciously choose between loyalty to his society & morality and his friend's freedom. He was even prepared to go to hell. That moment of choice is one of the great moments in American literature. |

# Chapter 3 - Reading: Informational Text

The objective of the Reading Informational Text standards is to ensure that the student is able to rea and comprehend informational texts (such as history/social studies, science, and technical texts) re lated to Grade 6.

To help students master the necessary skills, information to help the student understand the concept related to the standard is given. Along with this, we encourage the student to go through the resourc es available online on EdSearch to gain an in depth understanding of these concepts. The EdSearc page for each lesson can be accessed with the help of the url or the QR code provided.

A small map is provided after each passage or text in which the student can enter the details a understood from the literary text. Doing this will help the student to refer to key points that help i answering the questions with ease.

# Chapter 3

## Lesson 1: Cite Textual Evidence to Support Analysis

*Let us understand the concept with an example.*

Once upon a time there were four boys living in the same town who were good friends. One boy was very clever but he did not like books. His name was Good Sense. The other boys were not very clever but they had read every book in the school.

After they graduated from high school, they decided to take a hike in the woods. While hiking, they came upon the bones of a lion. The three of them who were book lovers decided to put the bones together to make a lion's skeleton. Good Sense told them: "A lion is a dangerous animal and if brought to life will kill us. Don't make a lion."

But the three boys disregarded his advice and started assembling a lion. Good Sense was very clever. While his friends were busy making the lion, he climbed up a tree to save himself. No sooner had the three boys finished constructing the lion and giving it life than it pounced on them and ate them up. Good Sense waited in the tree until the lion left, then walked home very sad at what had happened to his friends.

**Here is what you might write.**

Although this is a fantasy (imaginative fiction, not capable of happening), I have inferred an important message from this story. The message is: While we accept that book learning can be useful, it should be combined with common sense, which can be more valuable when facing actual situations, especially dangerous situations.

This story is proof of this. Good Sense survived because he used common sense, which led him to guess accurately what would happen when the lion's bones were assembled and the lion was given life. His common sense saved his life. The other three boys, while they had the knowledge to assemble the lion's bones (probably by reading books about lions), did not have the common sense to guess what would happen if the lion was brought back to life, even when warned by Good Sense. They did not survive.

**You can scan the QR code given below or use the url to access additional EdSearch resources including videos and mobile apps related to *Cite Textual Evidence*.**

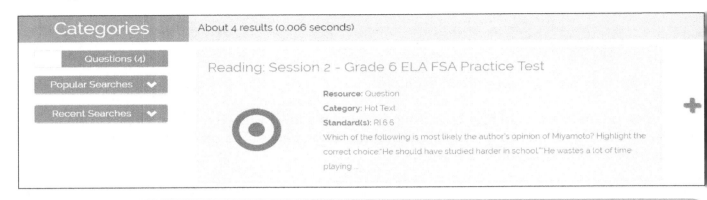

| Categories | About 4 results (0.006 seconds) |
|---|---|
| Questions (4) | |
| Popular Searches ⌄ | Reading: Session 2 - Grade 6 ELA FSA Practice Test |
| Recent Searches ⌄ | |

**Resource:** Question
**Category:** Hot Text
**Standard(s):** RI.6.6
Which of the following is most likely the author's opinion of Miyamoto? Highlight the correct choice"He should have studied harder in school""He wastes a lot of time playing ...

 Search

## *Cite Textual Evidence*

| URL | QR Code |
|---|---|
| http://www.lumoslearning.com/a/ri61 |  |

Everywhere around us, there are millions of tiny living things called germs. They are so tiny that they can be seen only under the most powerful microscope. Some of these germs are no wider than twenty-five thousandths of an inch!

Louis Pasteur, the great French scientist, was the first to prove that germs exist. The germs in the air can be counted. The number of germs around us, especially in crowded rooms, is tremendous. Certain scientists counted 42,000 germs in approximately one cubic meter of air in a picture gallery when it was empty. But when the gallery was crowded with people, they found nearly 5,000,000 germs in the same place. In the open-air, germs are less abundant. There are fewer germs in the country air than in town air. We see at once how important it is, therefore, to live as much as possible in the open air, and for the rooms, we live in to always be well ventilated by fresh air.

**1. According to the passage, where will you find more germs?**

Ⓐ  In crowded spaces
Ⓑ  In the country
Ⓒ  In hospitals
Ⓓ  In empty rooms

**2. Which of the following statements can be concluded after reading the passage?**

Ⓐ  Louis Pasteur liked counting germs.
Ⓑ  Germs are too small to be seen.
Ⓒ  People have germs.
Ⓓ  Fresher air has fewer germs.

George Washington was the first and most popular U.S. President. He was the only one elected by a unanimous vote. It is often said of him that he was "first in war, first in peace, and first in the hearts of his countrymen." Washington led comparatively untrained and ill-equipped American soldiers to victory over the well-trained British in the Revolutionary War. As soon as the Constitution was ratified, he was chosen to be president.

Many of the generals who had fought under Washington did not believe that the 13 colonies could cooperate to form a single country without the strong leadership of a king. They approached him, saying that they would support him as King George I of the United States. Washington was dismayed at the idea, and asked the generals to promise never to mention it again. He served two terms as president and refused a third term, retiring to his farm in Virginia. When England's King George heard that Washington had voluntarily given up the power of the presidency, he said, "If that is true, he is the greatest man in history."

3. **How does the author show that George Washington is a great man?**

   Ⓐ He led untrained soldiers into battle.
   Ⓑ He was unanimously elected president.
   Ⓒ He voluntarily gave up the power of the presidency.
   Ⓓ All of the above.

4. **Based upon the above story about George Washington, which of the following words bes describe him?**

   Ⓐ Smart
   Ⓑ Power hungry
   Ⓒ Strong leader
   Ⓓ Kind

5. **According to the text, why was Washington considered the most popular president?**

   Ⓐ King George I said, "He is the greatest man in history."
   Ⓑ He was elected president by a unanimous vote.
   Ⓒ He wanted to be a powerful man and king.
   Ⓓ He was the first president

When Westinghouse, the inventor of the air brake, was working on his great invention, he made a application for a trial of his device to the New York Central Railroad. Vanderbilt, the president of th railroad, thought the inventor's claims were absurd. In comparison with the hand brake then in use Westinghouse stated that one man instead of two could operate his brake and that his brake woul stop a fifty-car train in fifty yards, compared to a sixty-five car train in two hundred yards with han brakes.

It is said that Vanderbilt roared with laughter. The idea of stopping a train of cars using airpowe appeared to be a joke to him. So, he returned the letter, with these words scribbled at the bottom: " have no time to waste on fools."

The young inventor next turned to the head of another railroad. He was younger and more progres sive than his New York rival. He sent for Westinghouse, listened to his explanations, and even ac vanced him money to continue his experiments. Best of all, he tested the new brake and found the Westinghouse was on the right track. Vanderbilt, hearing of the test, regretted his curt dismissal of th idea. He wrote a courteous note to the inventor, fixing a time for an interview. The note came bac with the brief inscription: "I have no time to waste on fools," George Westinghouse.

**6. Which of the following statements can be concluded after reading the passage above?**

Ⓐ  Westinghouse was thankful Vanderbilt helped him.
Ⓑ  Vanderbilt regretted not listening to Westinghouse's ideas.
Ⓒ  Westinghouse was a successful train engineer.
Ⓓ  Westinghouse's invention was foolish.

Michael Jordan was the greatest basketball player of all time. When he played for the Chicago Bulls, they had one winning season after another. He scored more than 100 points in 1,108 games, won two Olympic gold medals, and was ranked #1 by ESPN Magazine. Chosen for the NBA All-Stars 14 times, Jordan was ten times the scoring champ, five times the Most Valuable Player, and six times the scoring champ of the NBA. When he began losing his hair, he shaved his head completely and started a fashion trend for other players. He was chosen to make an animated movie called "Space Jam" with Bugs Bunny. No other player has come close to those achievements.

**7. According to passage, which of the following is NOT a reason why Michael Jordan is considered the greatest basketball player of all time?**

Ⓐ  Michael Jordan shaved his head.
Ⓑ  Michael Jordan won two gold medals in the Olympics.
Ⓒ  Michael Jordan scored more than 100 points in 1,108 games.
Ⓓ  Michael Jordan was the Most Valuable Player five times.

**8. Why did the author write this passage about Michael Jordan?**

Ⓐ  To describe about how Michael Jordan made a movie with Bugs Bunny.
Ⓑ  To show what a great basketball player Michael Jordan is.
Ⓒ  To give readers Michael Jordan's life story.
Ⓓ  To tell people what it is like to be a famous basketball player.

Most of the planets in our solar system have moons. Saturn has the most, with eighteen moons. Jupiter has sixteen; Uranus has fifteen. Earth has only one, but our moon has a big influence on the lives of humans on Earth. In ancient times, people believed that moonlight could affect people's brains. The Latin word for the moon was Luna. Words like "lunatic" and "looney" come from that idea. Many people still believe that more babies are born and more people die when the moon is full. Scientific studies that have been done to see whether the numbers of births and deaths actually increase when there is a full moon show that there is no increase. The gravitational pull of the moon affects the tides in the ocean, but does not seem to affect the births and deaths of people. Does the full moon cause people to fall in love? That's another question!

**9. What, according to the passage, has a "looney" effect on people?**

Ⓐ  The tides
Ⓑ  Saturn
Ⓒ  Babies
Ⓓ  The moon

**10. After reading this passage, what inference can you make? Circle the correct answer choice.**

Ⓐ  People believe the moon causes crazy things to happen.
Ⓑ  Moonlight from the Earth's moon is less powerful because we only have one moon.
Ⓒ  People believe that births, deaths, and love is not influenced by the moon.
Ⓓ  Earth's moon is bigger than Jupiter's.

How does the body know to breathe and move?
The central nervous system tells the body what to do.
The nervous system is made up of nerves, the spinal cord and the brain.

**11. From the above lines, we can infer that the nervous system is the _____ of the human body.**
**Fill in the blank by choosing the correct option from among the 4 options given below.**

Ⓐ  digesting system
Ⓑ  breathing system
Ⓒ  circulatory system
Ⓓ  control system

# Chapter 3

## Lesson 2: Central Idea of Text

*Publisher's Note: to identify the main idea(s) or theme of written text, you have to figure out what the author considers the most important purpose, message or lesson that he/she wants you to recognize. It could be a lesson in morals or a call for you to take some action or just to entertain you. Key details are used to further explain things about the main idea(s). Summarizing the text means writing only the main ideas.*

Example: You have been assigned to read the following article, and write text that meets what the standard requires.

Scientists tell us that changes in our climate are happening. Average temperatures around the world are getting higher. The planet's average surface temperature has risen about 2.0 degrees Fahrenheit since the late 19th century. The warmest year on record was 2016; eight months were the warmest on record. The number of warm days in a year has increased while the number of cold days has decreased. This is called global warming.

Because of the rise in temperature, the ice caps in Greenland and Antarctica are melting and have caused sea levels to rise 8" in the last 100 years; glaciers are shrinking; ocean water temperatures are rising. Carbon dioxide levels in the air have risen from an average of 300 ppm (parts per million) to 400 ppm, the highest levels ever. Carbon dioxide forms a blanket above the earth that traps heat, an additional contributor to global warming.

Studies by scientists point out that global warming is having bad effects on humans, animals and plants. Carbon dioxide reduces air quality, which is not healthy for humans and animals to breathe. Water is essential for living creatures; without enough water they die. Global warming decreases the amount of water on the planet. Some creatures cannot adapt quickly to changes in climates and will die, and those that migrate can be forced to change their migration patterns.

Why is global warming happening? Ninety seven percent of global scientists think this is happening because of activities by humans. Our use of fuels from fossils, such as oil, gas and coal, are major causes, and our manufacturing activities are another cause.

What can we do about it? We need your help to convince our government and companies that use chemicals to manufacture their products to agree to rules that minimize the release of harmful chemicals into the air. Please sign up to help us at: (assume that the author provides a link to a signup form).

Your assignment: To identify the central (main) idea(s) in the article and explain how the author use key details (reasons and evidence) to support his/her main idea(s), and then to summarize the article

**The following is an example of what you might write.**

The author claims that global warming is happening; this is one main idea in the article. The secon main idea is to convince you to sign up with an organization that tries to convince government an certain companies to minimize the release of chemicals into the air.

To support the claim that global warming is happening, the author presents data proving that glob temperatures have been rising, major ice caps are melting and carbon dioxide levels in the atmo sphere have increased, all as a result of global warming.

The author states that science studies show that global warming is having bad effects on human animals and plants. The author gives several key details to support this statement, such as a reductio (decrease) in air quality, reduction in fresh water supplies, inability (or not able to do something) some creatures to adapt to changes in climate and disruption (change) of migration patterns.

You might summarize the article this way: Global warming is happening. Scientists have conducte studies that prove this using actual data, and the article gives examples. Global warming has harm ful effects on human, animal and plant life on Earth. The article gives examples. The author reques your help in combating global warming and provides a link to a website that provides informatio on how you can help.

**You can scan the QR code given below or use the url to access additional EdSearch resource including videos and mobile apps related to *Central Idea of Text*.**

ed)Search          ***Central Idea of Text***

| URL | QR Code |
|---|---|
| http://www.lumoslearning.com/a/ri62 | |

1. Books were hard to get for the mountain men among the western settlers.
2. Sometimes a mountain man would carry a single battered book with him for years.
3. Some of the men had Bibles, and even more had Shakespeare's plays.
4. Shakespeare was a favorite with mountain men, even if they could not read.
5. When they found someone who could read, he was often asked to read one of Shakespeare's plays to a group over a campfire.
6. There were mountain men who could not sign their own names, but could quote passages of Shakespeare by heart.

## 1. Part A
**Which sentence best shows the central idea of this paragraph?**

Ⓐ Sentence #1
Ⓑ Sentence #6
Ⓒ Sentence #3
Ⓓ Sentence #5

**Part B**
**Which two sentences best support the answer to Part A**

Ⓐ Sentences #2 and #6
Ⓑ Sentences #3 and #5
Ⓒ Sentences #1 and #2
Ⓓ Sentences #3 and #6

## 2. Which sentence does not directly support the central idea?

Ⓐ Sentence #2
Ⓑ Sentence #3
Ⓒ Sentence #5
Ⓓ Sentence #6

The rainforest has many layers. Different plants and animals live in each layer. Some layers get more sunlight than others.

## 3. Which is the central idea of the passage?

Ⓐ We should take care of the rainforest.
Ⓑ There are many layers in the rainforest.
Ⓒ Some layers get sunlight.
Ⓓ Rainforests are too wet.

**4. A main central is _____ and then has details that follow to support it.**

- Ⓐ Specific
- Ⓑ General
- Ⓒ Both specific and general
- Ⓓ Very detailed

**5. The purpose of supporting details is _____.**

- Ⓐ To give you a conclusion
- Ⓑ To tell you the point of view of the story
- Ⓒ To tell the central idea
- Ⓓ To give more information to support the central idea

1. Homophones, homographs, and homonyms have different definitions.
2. Homophones are words that sound the same, but are spelled differently and have different meanings.
3. "The golfer drank tea before tee time."
4. Homographs are words that are spelled the same, but are not pronounced the same way.
5. "The artist is planning to record a new record."
6. When two homographs are also homophones, they are called homonyms: word pairs that are spelled the same and pronounced the same way.
7. "He felt fine after he paid the fine."
8. "You can drink juice from a can."
9. You can remember homographs by remembering that "graph" means to write, as in autograph.
10. You can remember homophones by remembering that "phone" means sound, as in telephone.

**6. What is the author's probable purpose in including Sentences #9 and #10?**

- Ⓐ Sentences #9 and #10 help the reader remember the definition of homograph and homophone.
- Ⓑ Sentences #9 and #10 help the reader see the difference between a homograph and a homophone.
- Ⓒ Sentences #9 and #10 help the reader understand the definition of a homonym.
- Ⓓ Sentences #9 and #10 help the reader understand the difference between a homophone and a homonym.

**7. Which sentence is the central idea of the passage?**

Ⓐ  Sentence #1
Ⓑ  Sentence #4
Ⓒ  Sentence #6
Ⓓ  Sentence #10

**8. Which sentence is a supporting detail for Sentence #2?**

Ⓐ  Sentence #3
Ⓑ  Sentence #4
Ⓒ  Sentence #5
Ⓓ  Sentence #10

**9. What sentence is supported by detail in Sentence #7?**

Ⓐ  Sentence #8
Ⓑ  Sentence #6
Ⓒ  Sentence #7
Ⓓ  Sentence #5

Everywhere around us there are millions of tiny living things called germs. They are so tiny that they can be seen only under the most powerful microscope. Some of these germs are no wider than twenty-five thousandth's of an inch!

Louis Pasteur, the great French scientist, was the first to prove that germs exist. The germs in the air can be counted. The number of germs around us, especially in crowded rooms, is tremendous. Certain scientists counted 42,000 germs in approximately one cubic meter of air in a picture gallery when it was empty. But when the gallery was crowded with people, they found nearly 5,000,000 germs in the same place. In the open air germs are less abundant. There are fewer germs in country air than in town air. We see at once how important it is, therefore, to live as much as possible in the open air, and for the rooms we live in to always be well ventilated by fresh air.

**10. Part A**
   **What is the above passage primarily about?**

Ⓐ  The French scientist Louis Pasteur
Ⓑ  The germs
Ⓒ  The most powerful microscope
Ⓓ  Living in the country

**Part B**
**What do you understand by reading the first paragraph of the above passage?**

Ⓐ Everywhere around us there are millions of tiny living things.
Ⓑ They can be seen only under a microscope
Ⓒ They are called germs
Ⓓ All of the above

Washing clothes is a difficult task. The skill has to be learned and mastered. It is a tedious and tiresome process, which often discourages a person from going through the exercise. In spite of the availability of modern detergent powders, it remains a difficult task. An expert knows which part of the dress need special care and attention. The collars of shirts and the seat and pockets of pants are generally dirtier than the other parts. But to wash well, what you require most is patience and the knowledge of the texture and quality of the cloth you are washing so that you can differentiate between clothes which can be put in warm water and which must never be washed in hot water. Woolens, silken and cotton clothes need different types of washing and detergents. One must have proper knowledge of these before washing clothes.

**12. What is the above passage about?**

# Chapter 3

## Lesson 3: Analyze How People, Events, or Ideas are Presented in Text

*Let us understand the concept with an example.*

In year's past, hand brakes were used to stop wagons, carriages, cars and trucks, and trains. Today hydraulic brakes have replaced hand brakes in cars and small trucks (except for emergency brakes), and air brakes have replaced hand brakes in large trucks and in trains. How did the air brake come about? Read on.

In March 5, 1868, an engineer named George Westinghouse patented an innovative air brake that was superior to an existing model of air brake and to hand brakes. While Westinghouse was working in this invention, he sent a letter to the New York Central Railroad requesting a trial of his air brake. After all, it had the advantages of only requiring one man, not two, to operate it and could stop a train in a shorter distance than the hand brakes currently in use. But the company president, Mr. Vanderbilt, thought the idea was ridiculous and scribbled "I have no time to waste on fools" at the bottom, and sent the letter back.

Mr. Westinghouse did not give up his idea. Instead, he approached another railroad whose president was more progressive. This president accepted the idea, loaned Westinghouse money to finish development, and arranged for a test, which proved Westinghouse's concept was correct. Upon hearing about the successful test, Mr. Vanderbilt realized he had made a mistake and wrote a courteous note to Westinghouse setting a date for an interview. Mr. Westinghouse returned the note, after scribbling at the bottom "I have no time to waste on fools."

**Here is what you might write.**

The central idea discussed in the text is the invention of an air brake to replace hand brakes on trains. The idea was invented by an engineer named George Westinghouse. He contacted a railroad company and persuaded its president to lend him money to fully develop and test his invention. It was successful. Besides information about this invention, what also makes this story interesting are two anecdotes. The first tells about the insulting note written by the well-known president of the New York Central Railroad that rejected his request for a trial; the words he used were "I have no time to waste on fools." The second tells about the president of the New York Central Railroad realizing his mistake and inviting Mr. Westinghouse to meet with him, and Mr. Westinghouse scrawling a note on the invitation rejecting it using the same language that the railroad president had used - "I have no time to waste on fools."

The fact that this insulting rejection from the New York Central Railroad president did not stop Mr. Westinghouse from continuing with his idea is a credit to him for his belief in his idea and his persistence.

You can scan the QR code given below or use the url to access additional EdSearch resources including videos and mobile apps related to **Analyze How People, Events, or Ideas are Presented in Text.**

## Analyze How People, Events, or Ideas are Presented in Text

| URL | QR Code |
|-----|---------|
| http://www.lumoslearning.com/a/ri63 |  |

Everywhere around us, there are millions of tiny living things called germs. They are so tiny that they can be seen only under the most powerful microscope. Some of these germs are no wider than twenty-five thousandths of an inch!

Louis Pasteur, the great French scientist, was the first to prove that germs exist. The germs in the air can be counted. The number of germs around us, especially in crowded rooms, is tremendous. Certain scientists counted 42,000 germs in approximately one cubic meter of air in a picture gallery when it was empty. But when the gallery was crowded with people, they found nearly 5,000,000 germs in the same place. In the open-air germs are less abundant. There are fewer germs in the country air than in town air. We see at once how important it is, therefore, to live as much as possible in the open air, and for the rooms, we live in to always be well ventilated by fresh air.

**After reading the story, enter the details in the map below. This will help you answer the questions with ease.**

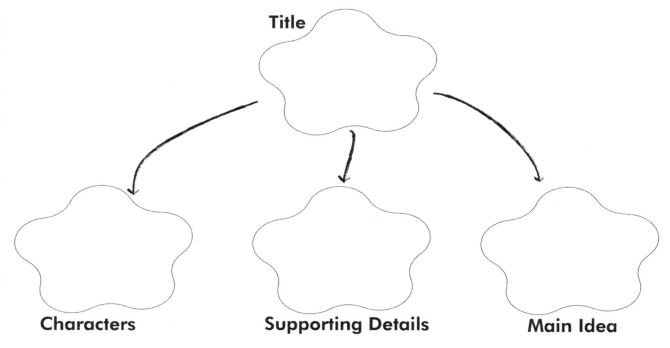

. **What is the central idea of the above passage?**

Ⓐ   Louis Pasteur was a great French scientist.
Ⓑ   Germs are everywhere.
Ⓒ   Germs are small.
Ⓓ   Germs can be counted.

**2. Which of the following details does NOT support the central idea of the passage?**

Ⓐ  Germs are tiny and can only be seen using powerful microscopes.
Ⓑ  There are fewer germs in open air.
Ⓒ  The more people you are around, the sicker you will become.
Ⓓ  Germs are living things.

George Washington was the first and most popular U.S. President. He was the only one elected by unanimous vote. It is often said of him that he was "first in war, first in peace, and first in the heart of his countrymen."

Washington led comparatively untrained and ill-equipped American soldiers to victory over the well-trained British in the Revolutionary War. As soon as the Constitution was ratified, he was chosen to be President.

Many of the generals who had fought under Washington did not believe that the 13 colonies could cooperate to form a single country without the strong leadership of a king. They approached him saying that they would support him as King George I of the United States. Washington was dismayed at the idea, and asked the generals to promise never to mention it again. He served two terms as President and refused a third term, retiring to his farm in Virginia. When England's King George heard that Washington had voluntarily given up the power of the presidency, he said, "If that is true, he is the greatest man in history."

**After reading the story, enter the details in the map below. This will help you answer the questions with ease.**

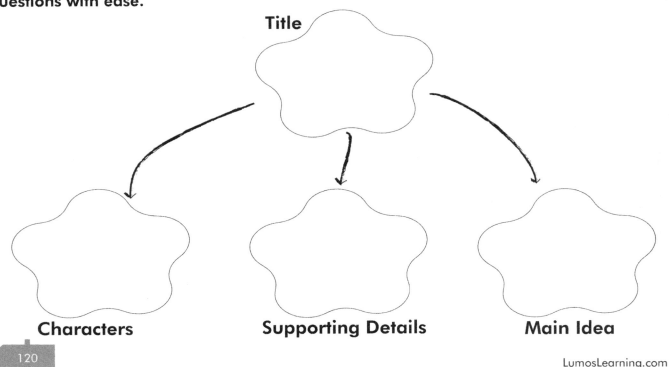

Title

Characters          Supporting Details          Main Idea

## 3. What is the central idea of the above passage?

Ⓐ George Washington refused a third term as president.
Ⓑ King George said that Washington is a great man.
Ⓒ George Washington was also known as King George I of the United States.
Ⓓ George Washington was a general and the first president of United States of America.

## 4. Based upon the above story about George Washington, which of the following words best describe him?

Ⓐ Smart
Ⓑ Power hungry
Ⓒ Strong leader
Ⓓ Kind

When Michael Jordan played for the Chicago Bulls, they had one winning season after another. He scored more than 100 points in 1,108 games, won two Olympic gold medals, and was ranked #1 by ESPN Magazine. Chosen for the NBA All-Stars 14 times, Jordan was ten times the scoring champ, five times the Most Valuable Player, and six times the scoring champ of the NBA. When he began losing his hair, he shaved his head completely and started a fashion trend for other players. He was chosen to make an animated movie called "Space Jam" with Bugs Bunny. No other player has come close to those achievements.

## 5. Which of the following would be the best introductory, or topic sentence, for the above passage?

Ⓐ Michael Jordan is often considered to be the greatest basketball player of all time.
Ⓑ Michael Jordan loves playing basketball.
Ⓒ When Michael Jordan isn't playing basketball he is starring in movies.
Ⓓ Michael Jordan won games, medals, and awards as a basketball player.

## 6. Which of the following sentences best supports the central idea of the passage?

Ⓐ Michael Jordan was scoring champ of the NBA six times.
Ⓑ Michael Jordan scored more than 100 points in 1,108 games.
Ⓒ Michael Jordan is best friends with Bugs Bunny.
Ⓓ Both A and B.

When Westinghouse, the inventor of the air brake, was working on his great invention, he made an application for a trial of his device to the New York Central Railroad. Vanderbilt, the president of the railroad, thought the inventor's claims were absurd. In comparison with the hand brake then in use, Westinghouse stated that one man instead of two could operate his brake and that his brake would stop a fifty-car train in fifty yards, compared to a sixty-five car train in two hundred yards with hand brakes.

It is said that Vanderbilt roared with laughter. The idea of stopping a train of cars by wind appeared to him to be a joke. So he returned the letter, with these words scribbled at the bottom: "I have no time to waste on fools."

The young inventor next turned to the head of another railroad. He was younger and more progressive than his New York rival. He sent for Westinghouse, listened to his explanations, and even advanced him money to continue his experiments. Best of all, he tested the new brake and found that Westinghouse was on the right track. Vanderbilt, hearing of the test, regretted his curt dismissal of the idea. He wrote a courteous note to the inventor, fixing a time for an interview. The note came back with the brief inscription: "I have no time to waste on fools," George Westinghouse.

**7. What is the above passage mostly about?**

Ⓐ Railroads during the 1800s
Ⓑ Vanderbilt and his dislike for fools
Ⓒ Air brakes
Ⓓ George Westinghouse's invention

**8. How did Westinghouse react to Vanderbilt's dismissal of his idea?**

Ⓐ Westinghouse gave up.
Ⓑ Westinghouse kept trying.
Ⓒ Westinghouse got mad at Vanderbilt.
Ⓓ Westinghouse decided to try inventing something else.

**9. What kind of person does the passage illustrate George Westinghouse to be?**

Ⓐ Foolish
Ⓑ Smart
Ⓒ Determined
Ⓓ Courteous

Books were hard to get for the mountain men among the western settlers. Sometimes a mountain man would carry a single battered book with him for years. Some of the men had Bibles, and even more had Shakespeare's plays. Shakespeare was a favorite with mountain men, even if they could not read. When they found someone who could read, he was often asked to read one of Shakespeare's plays to a group over a campfire. There were mountain men who could not sign their own names, but could quote passages of Shakespeare by heart.

**10. How does the author of the above passage show that books were important to mountain men?**

Ⓐ Books were hard for mountain men to get.
Ⓑ Some mountain men had Shakespeare's plays.
Ⓒ Some mountain men could quote Shakespeare.
Ⓓ Not all mountain men could read.

Washing clothes is a difficult task. The skill has to be learned and mastered. It is a tedious and tiresome process, which often discourages a person from going through the exercise. In spite of the availability of modern detergent powders, it remains a difficult task. An expert knows which parts of the clothing needs special care and attention. The collars of shirts and the seat and pockets of pants are generally dirtier than the other parts. But to wash well, what you require most is patience and the knowledge of the texture and quality of the cloth you are washing so that you can differentiate between clothes which can be put in warm water and clothes which must never be washed in hot water. Woolens, silk and cotton clothes need different types of washing and detergents. One must have proper knowledge of this before washing clothes.

**11. How does the author of the above passage illustrate that washing clothes is a difficult task? Circle the correct answer choice.**

Ⓐ By discussing the different types of washing machines.
Ⓑ By pointing out that certain parts of clothing need special care and attention.
Ⓒ By talking about all the different laundry detergent options.
Ⓓ By explaining how time consuming laundry can be.

# Chapter 3

## Lesson 4: Determine Technical Meanings

**Definitions:**

1. Figurative: Figurative language is language where the meaning of a word or phrase is different from the literal (primary or strict or dictionary) meaning. Another way of defining figurative is: using language that has another meaning besides its normal definition.

2. Connotative: Connotative meanings suggest that there is an associated or secondary meaning of a word or expression, in addition to its primary meaning, that the reader or listener will have to identify himself/herself, since it is not stated in the text.

3. Technical: language (jargon) that is connected with one specific subject or used in one specific activity or job.

*Let us understand the concept with an example.*

### The Ant and the Grasshopper Aesop's Fable

In a field one summer's day, a grasshopper was hopping about, chirping and singing to its heart's content. A group of ants walked by, grunting as they struggled to carry plump kernels of corn. "Where are you going with those heavy things?" asked the grasshopper.

Without stopping, the first ant replied, "To our ant hill. This is the third kernel I've delivered today."
"Why not come and sing with me," teased the grasshopper, "instead of working so hard?"
"We are helping to store food for the winter," said the ant, "and think you should do the same."
"Winter is far away and it is a glorious day to play," sang the grasshopper. But the ants went on their way and continued their hard work.

The weather soon turned cold. All the food lying in the field was covered with a thick white blanket of snow that even the grasshopper could not dig through.

Soon the grasshopper found himself dying of hunger. He staggered to the ants' hill and saw them handing out corn from the stores they had collected in the summer. He begged them for something to eat.
"What?" cried the ants in surprise, "haven't you stored anything away for the winter?"

"What in the world were you doing all last summer?"

"I didn't have time to store any food," complained the grasshopper, "I was so busy playing music that before I knew it the summer was gone."

The ants shook their head in disgust, turned their backs on the grasshopper, and went on with their work.

**This is what you might write.**

The central idea of the story is to teach the lesson "always be prepared," although the author never actually says that. Instead, the author uses the conversations and actions of the grasshopper and the ants to teach the lesson "always be prepared," and hopes that you will figure out the lesson yourself after reading the story. Because the author never actually states the lesson, but uses the characters as examples to show the lesson, the author is using a figurative language technique called allegory. Another example of using figurative language in this story is an epiphany, which was the moment in the story when the grasshopper realizes, to his despair, that he made a huge mistake by playing in the summer when he should have been getting and storing food for the winter.

A third example of using figurative language is the fable. A fable is a concise and brief story intended to provide a moral lesson at the end; in this case, the lesson "always be prepared."

The story has a connotative meaning. It is the lesson "always be prepared," which the reader has to figure out after reading a story about ants gathering food and a grasshopper watching them while playing, because the author never mentions it.

There only technical phrase in this story is "ant hill," which is only used when writing about ants.

**You can scan the QR code given below or use the url to access additional EdSearch resources including videos and mobile apps related to *Determine Technical Meanings*.**

## Determine Technical Meanings

| URL | QR Code |
| --- | --- |
| http://www.lumoslearning.com/a/ri64 |  |

**1. What is a synonym of a word?**

Ⓐ  A word that has the same meaning as the given word.
Ⓑ  A word that has the opposite meaning of a given word.
Ⓒ  A word that has the same spelling as the given word.
Ⓓ  A word that has the same pronunciation as the given word.

**2. Which of the following statements is true about antonyms?**

Ⓐ  They have the same meaning as the given word.
Ⓑ  They are the definitions of a given word.
Ⓒ  They have the same sounds as a given word.
Ⓓ  They are the opposites of a given word.

The words "minute" (time) and "minute" (extremely small) are pronounced differently and have different meanings.

**3. These types of words are called _____.**

Ⓐ  Homophones
Ⓑ  Homonyms
Ⓒ  Homographs
Ⓓ  Homo-words

**4. Which of the choices below is an example of an "antonym?"**

Ⓐ  Clever, crazy
Ⓑ  Pretty, beautiful
Ⓒ  Narrow, skinny
Ⓓ  Abundant, scarce

**5. Which of the choices below is an example of synonyms?**

Ⓐ  mini, tiny
Ⓑ  clever, foolish
Ⓒ  good, bad
Ⓓ  soggy, dry

**6. Choose the correct set of antonyms from the following.**

Ⓐ courteous, kind
Ⓑ regretted, refused
Ⓒ brief, small
Ⓓ stopped, started

**7. Choose the set of rhyming words from the following.**

Ⓐ fresh, air
Ⓑ space, spread
Ⓒ worms, germs
Ⓓ breathe, breath

**8. A group of words that share the same spelling and pronunciation but have different meanings is called a _____.**

Ⓐ Synonym
Ⓑ Homonym
Ⓒ Syllable
Ⓓ Consonant

**9. Which of the following statements defines homophones?**

Ⓐ The words that have the same meaning and different spellings.
Ⓑ The words that have the same sound but different meanings.
Ⓒ The words that have the same sound but have different meanings and spellings.
Ⓓ The words that do not have the same sound but have the same meaning and spelling.

**10. Identify the correct set of homophones from the following.**

Ⓐ mustard, mustered
Ⓑ loan, lone
Ⓒ lumbar, lumber
Ⓓ both A and B

## 11. Part A

A word that has the same meaning or nearly the same meaning as another word is (an) _____.

Ⓐ Antonym
Ⓑ Synonym
Ⓒ Homophone
Ⓓ Rhyme

### Part B

A word that has the opposite meaning to another is a (an) _____.

Ⓐ Antonym
Ⓑ Synonym
Ⓒ Homophone
Ⓓ Rhyme

# Chapter 3

## Lesson 5: Structure of Text

*Let us understand the concept with an example.*

Over the course of history in the United States, necessity and economics have combined to change the way we transport cargo, which can be living creatures (people, animals and plants) or nonliving items. When the colonies were settled, walking or riding horses or using horses, oxen or mules with carriages, stagecoaches and wagons were the common forms of transportation on land. But these were relatively slow, limited in the number of passengers or cargo they could carry, and cumbersome when having to deal with natural forces like streams, mountains, forests, heavy snow, heavy rain and the resulting mud. Horses require a lot of care - food, water, shelter, horseshoes, harnesses and saddles.

Then someone harnessed the power of steam. The first commercially successful steam engine with pistons and cylinders was introduced in 1712. Steam engines were used in a variety of ways, from powering factory machines to locomotives. Steam-driven locomotives, which used plentiful coal and water, could transport many more people and cargo than animals pulling wagon, at a greater speed over a long distance. All that was needed were rails (instead of roads), which required a lot of initial effort, but once built, required much less effort to maintain.

However the benefits brought by the steam engine were exceeded by the introductions of two other forms of fuel: gasoline and diesel. Engines powered by gasoline appeared in the late 1700s. Once refined from oil, gasoline was a much easier fuel to use in automobiles and other vehicles than steam. In 1892, a patent for the first diesel engine was applied for. Diesel-powered engines increased the hauling power of trains and had the further advantage of not needing a fireman to keep shoveling coal into the boiler as with the steam-powered train. As gasoline and diesel engines improved, they became the principal engines used to power automobiles, trucks, buses, ships and trains.

In 1903, the first-heavier-than-air flight (balloons were considered lighter-than-air flights) by the Wright brothers ushered in the age of flight. While early aircraft were severely limited in the number of people or cargo they could carry, the development of more powerful gasoline engines increased the cargo capacity, speed and distance an aircraft could fly. The introduction of the jet engine increased these capabilities even more. Also, the gasoline engine was an important factor in making automobiles more useful than a horse, oxen or mule for transporting cargo. Some advantage of aircraft were the speed at which cargo could be transported, for the purpose of conducting business meetings, peaceful trade or warfare, and rescue missions.

Your assignment: select key sentences or paragraphs and show how they fit into the above article and contribute to the central ideas of the article.

The central idea of the article is expressed in the first sentence: "Over the course of history in the

United States, necessity and economics have combined to change the way we transport cargo…" The rest of the article gives proof to support this central idea.

The sentence "Then someone harnessed the power of steam" is a key sentence that acts as a transition from the period that relied primarily on horses, oxen and mules to the next time period and the next invention to improve transportation, the steam engine.

The sentence "But the benefits brought by the steam engine were exceeded by the introductions of two other forms of fuel: gasoline and diesel." transitions the reader to the next time period and transportation improvements - gasoline and diesel engines.

The next transition sentence was: "In 1903, the first-heavier-than-air flight (balloons were considered lighter-than-air flights) by the Wright brothers ushered in the age of flight." The gasoline engine made a major contribution to making aircraft functional for increased passenger and cargo loads. The final transition to an improvement in transportation was the introduction of the jet engine, which transitions transportation improvements forward to the present time.

The structure of the text in this article is chronological; that is, the methods used to transport cargo are described as they occurred over a period of time, from past to present. The methods to transport cargo progresses from the simplest (walking) to the most complex (jet engines). The sentence "When the colonies were settled, walking or riding horses or using horses, oxen or mules with carriages, stagecoaches and wagons were the common forms of transportation on land." is a key sentence that is the beginning of the time period covered by this article, and explains the simplest kinds of transportation.

https://edutrainingcenter.withgoogle.com/edu_assets/pdf/sample_gce_exam_questions.pdf

**You can scan the QR code given below or use the url to access additional EdSearch resources including videos and mobile apps related to *Structure of Text*.**

 **Structure of Text**

| URL | QR Code |
| --- | --- |
| http://www.lumoslearning.com/a/ri65 |  |

**1. Identify where the underlined sentence below belongs in the paragraph.**

<u>Start with the freshest bread you can find.</u>

I will tell you how to make a perfect peanut butter sandwich.
Take the two pieces of bread.
Add a good-sized scoop of crunchy peanut butter, and be sure to spread it on both pieces of bread.
Find a jar of your favorite jam.
Use slightly less jam than peanut butter, and spread it on only one slice of bread.
Put the two slices together and cut the sandwich in half. Enjoy.

Ⓐ   The missing sentence should be first.
Ⓑ   The missing sentence should be second.
Ⓒ   The missing sentence should be third.
Ⓓ   The missing sentence should be fourth.

**2. Identify where the underlined sentence below belongs in the paragraph.**

<u>During the pre-competition phase, continue the aerobic training, but add strength training and sprints.</u>

Training for tennis can be broken down into four phases.
During the preparation phase, work on aerobic fitness with jogging, swimming, or cycling as you train heavily on the specifics of tennis.
While competing, training can ease up except for the specifics of tennis.
For several weeks after competition, rest from playing tennis but keep up your fitness by playing other sports.

Ⓐ   The missing sentence should be first.
Ⓑ   The missing sentence should be second.
Ⓒ   The missing sentence should be third.
Ⓓ   The missing sentence should be fourth.

**3. Identify where the underlined sentence below belongs in the paragraph.**

**In French, the word means "rotten pot."**

Today we have spray cans for freshening the air, but it's more fun to make a potpourri. Potpourri were originally made in France by creating a mixture of flower petals and leaves that was allowed t sit in a crock for months. Today, many people still like to make potpourris from herbs and flower You can make your own from herbs and flowers from the garden.

- Ⓐ   The missing sentence should be first.
- Ⓑ   The missing sentence should be second.
- Ⓒ   The missing sentence should be third.
- Ⓓ   The missing sentence should be fourth.

**4. Arrange the sentences below in the most logical order.**

1. On the front of each cap is a white horse.
2. The caps also have the motto, "They fear no difficulty."
3. Officers can be identified by the crimson sash worn over their shoulders.
4. The tallest men have high bearskin caps.
5. The British troops present a colorful appearance.
6. Crowds gather to watch the elegant soldiers parade by.

- Ⓐ   6, 1, 2, 5, 4, 3
- Ⓑ   5, 3, 4, 1, 2, 6
- Ⓒ   5, 4, 3, 6, 1, 2
- Ⓓ   1, 2, 3, 4, 5, 6

**5. Arrange the sentences in the most logical order.**

1. Most farm families raised geese, so goose feathers were plentiful.
2. Colonists also used the feathers of wild turkeys and hawks.
3. Crow feathers were harder to collect, but were considered the best for making fine lines.
4. Colonists often made their quill pens from goose feathers.

- Ⓐ   4, 1, 2, 3
- Ⓑ   1, 2, 3, 4
- Ⓒ   3, 2, 1, 4
- Ⓓ   2, 3, 1, 4

## 6. Arrange the sentences in the most logical order.

1. Later, European traders spread pineapple growing to Africa and the Pacific Islands, including Hawaii.
2. The name was later changed to pineapple.
3. The name may come from the Dutch word for pinecone, which is pi jnappel.
4. Christopher Columbus was the first European to taste what he called "Indian pinecones."

- Ⓐ  4, 3, 2, 1
- Ⓑ  4, 1, 3, 2
- Ⓒ  1, 2, 3, 4
- Ⓓ  3, 2, 1, 4

When Westinghouse, the inventor of the air brake, was working on his great invention, he made an application for a trial of his device to the New York Central Railroad. Vanderbilt, the president of the railroad, thought the inventor's claims were absurd. In comparison with the hand brake then in use, Westinghouse stated that one man instead of two could operate his brake and that his brake would stop a fifty-car train in fifty yards, compared to a sixty-five car train in two hundred yards with hand brakes.

It is said that Vanderbilt roared with laughter. The idea of stopping a train of cars by wind appeared to him to be a joke. So he returned the letter, with these words scribbled at the bottom: "I have no time to waste on fools."

The young inventor next turned to the head of another railroad. He was younger and more progressive than his New York rival. He sent for Westinghouse, listened to his explanations, and even advanced him money to continue his experiments. Best of all, he tested the new brake and found that Westinghouse was on the right track. Vanderbilt, hearing of the test, regretted his curt dismissal of the idea. He wrote a courteous note to the inventor, fixing a time for an interview. The note came back with the brief inscription: "I have no time to waste on fools," George Westinghouse.

## 7. What kind of a writing piece is the above passage?

- Ⓐ  A personal narrative
- Ⓑ  A persuasive essay
- Ⓒ  An informative/expository passage
- Ⓓ  A journal entry

**8. Which of the following would turn the above passage into a personal narrative?**

Ⓐ  If the above passage was written by Westinghouse himself.
Ⓑ  If the author was President Vanderbilt and he wrote about George Westinghouse.
Ⓒ  If the author was a third person.
Ⓓ  None of the above

**9. What are the main parts of an essay?**

Ⓐ  A topic title
Ⓑ  An introduction to the topic
Ⓒ  Details about the topic and a conclusion to the topic
Ⓓ  All of the above

**10. What are the parts of a business letter?**

Ⓐ  The heading, the inside address
Ⓑ  The greeting, the body
Ⓒ  The complimentary close, the signature line
Ⓓ  All of the above

**11. The salutation in a business letter is what part of a letter?**

Ⓐ  Heading
Ⓑ  Closing
Ⓒ  Address and date
Ⓓ  Greeting

**12. Which of the following types of writing will most likely contain the most descriptive writing (imagery)? Circle the correct answer choice.**

Ⓐ  Letter of complaint to a store about a product that was faulty
Ⓑ  Personal narrative about a rodeo
Ⓒ  Descriptive paper about a winter day
Ⓓ  Informative/Expository paper about snow

## Chapter 3

## Lesson 6: Determine Author's Point of View

Here are two examples that represent use of the standard.

**Example 1:** The Board of Education in student Jennifer's town has asked for feedback from parents, teachers and students about the issue of whether students should be allowed to bring their smartphones and tablets to school to do school work in class.

In response to the request for feedback, Jennifer writes: We think allowing students to bring their smartphones and tablets to school to do school work in class is not a good idea. It provides too great an opportunity for students to play games or go on social media instead of focusing on performing assigned work. We favor the greater control that using school computers provides even though we sacrifice some efficiency.

Your assignment: Read Jennifer's letter and write what the standard requires.
Here is an example of what you might write.

Jennifer states her central idea, which is her point of view, in the first sentence "We think allowing students to bring their smartphones and tablets to school to do school work in class is not a good idea." Her purpose is to convince the Board of Education to prohibit students from bringing their smartphones and tablets to school. Her remaining text is intended to provide reasons in support of her main idea.

**Example 2:** Author Jimmy writes: "I am in favor of research that can create robots who think like humans. They could take the place of humans in customer support call centers by using technology that recognizes the caller's words, can match these words with pre-programmed solutions, and mimic a human voice in communicating these solutions to the caller. They would be available 24/7, because they would not take vacations or sick days."

Your assignment: Read Jimmy's letter and write what the standard requires.

Jimmy states his central idea, which is his point of view, in the first sentence, "I am in favor of research that can create robots who think like humans." His purpose is to convince you, the reader, that his position makes sense and to get you to support it. His remaining text gives reasons for supporting his main idea.

Let's assume that you disagree with Jimmy's position on this issue.
**Here is an example of what you might write.**

While I agree that robots do not take sick days or vacations, I do not agree with Jimmy's conclusion that "They could take the place of humans in call centers." I conclude that robots will not be able to handle requests for information as well as humans can, for several reasons. First, callers may have various accents when speaking English that a robot cannot understand. Second, a caller may not be able to clearly explain the problem, and may not use the keywords that a robot relies on to match to a solution. Third, a human can more accurately understand the need to transfer the caller to someone else, or to lookup additional information relating to the caller's request. Fourth, most callers would rather speak with a human than a robot for two reasons: more friendly feedback, and the capability of a human call center person to have a dialogue that goes beyond the initial question and response.

**You can scan the QR code given below or use the url to access additional EdSearch resources including videos and mobile apps related to *Determine Author's Point of View.***

 **Determine Author's Point of View**

| URL | QR Code |
| --- | --- |
| http://www.lumoslearning.com/a/ri66 |  |

Dogs are better pets than cats for many reasons. Dogs are a man's best friend and can learn tricks. Dogs will get you things when you ask them to. Dogs will go walking or running with you to help keep you in shape. Dogs like to cuddle and protect their owners.

**1. What is the purpose of the above passage?**

Ⓐ  To inform
Ⓑ  To explain
Ⓒ  To persuade
Ⓓ  To entertain

If you invent a new word and enough people like it, you may find it in the dictionary. Dictionaries add new words as they come into common use. The fancy word for a brand-new word is "neologism." In 2011, the Merriam-Webster Collegiate Dictionary added some neologisms you probably know, such as "tweet," "fist bump," and "social media."

Some of the new words may not be so familiar.

* "Planking" is a game of lying face down, hands at your sides, in the most unusual place you can think of, and having your picture taken and posted on the internet.
* A "bromance" is a close friendship – but not a romance – between two men.
* A "robocall" is a call made automatically by a machine repeating a taped message.
* A "helicopter parent" is one who hovers over their children, becoming much too involved in their lives.
* And "crowdsourcing"? That's the way many people can each do a little bit of a very large project. The country of Iceland, for example, is crowdsourcing a new constitution for their country, so if you have an idea about what they ought to include, you can go online and send them your suggestion.

At the same time new words are being added, old words that are no longer widely recognized are dropped from the dictionary. This year, the dictionary deleted the words "growlery" (a room where you can go to complain) and "brabble" (another word for squabble). If you haven't heard those words before, you probably won't miss them!

**2. What is the purpose of the passage above?**

Ⓐ  To inform
Ⓑ  To explain
Ⓒ  To persuade
Ⓓ  To entertain

I will tell you how to make a perfect peanut butter sandwich. Start with the freshest bread you can find. Take two pieces of bread. Add a good-sized scoop of crunchy peanut butter, and be sure to spread it on both pieces of bread. Find a jar of your favorite jam. Use slightly less jam than peanut butter, and spread it on only one slice of bread. Put the two slices together and cut the sandwich in half. Enjoy.

**3. Part A**
**What is the purpose of the passage above?**

Ⓐ To inform
Ⓑ To explain
Ⓒ To persuade
Ⓓ To entertain

**Part B**
**What point of view is the paragraph above told from?**

Ⓐ First person
Ⓑ Second person
Ⓒ Third person
Ⓓ Fourth person

Everywhere around us, there are millions of tiny living things called germs. They are so tiny that they can be seen only under the most powerful microscope. Some of these germs are no wider than twenty-five thousandths of an inch!

Louis Pasteur, the great French scientist, was the first to prove that germs exist. The germs in the air can be counted. The number of germs around us, especially in crowded rooms, is tremendous. Certain scientists counted 42,000 germs in approximately one cubic meter of air in a picture gallery when it was empty. But when the gallery was crowded with people, they found nearly 5,000,000 germs in the same place. In the open-air, germs are less abundant. There are fewer germs in the country air than in town air. We see at once how important it is, therefore, to live as much as possible in the open air, and for the rooms, we live in to always be well ventilated by fresh air.

**4. What is the purpose of the passage above?**

Ⓐ To inform
Ⓑ To explain
Ⓒ To persuade
Ⓓ To entertain

Football is the most exciting sport. During a football game, two teams of eleven players battle to reach the end zone. During the game, the players try to catch or run with the ball without being tackled by the opposing team. Sometimes players jump over each other, break tackles, and run as fast as lightning. Football fans cheer extremely loud when their team reaches the end zone. There is never a dull moment in football.

**5. What is the purpose of the passage above?**

Ⓐ  To convince readers to go to a football game.
Ⓑ  To tell a story about what happened at a football game.
Ⓒ  To explain to readers about what happens at a football game.
Ⓓ  To help the reader understand why to never attend a football game.

Eating carrots, broccoli, and string beans are good for you. Making sure to have healthy vegetables in your diet is important. Some people think eating vegetables at one meal is good enough, but it isn't; you should eat vegetables at least 3 meals a day.

**6. What is the purpose of the passage above?**

Ⓐ  To convince the reader to eat more vegetables.
Ⓑ  To give information about different types of vegetables.
Ⓒ  To tell about a cartoon where the characters are played by vegetables.
Ⓓ  The help the reader understand there is nothing important about vegetables.

George Washington was the first and most popular U.S. President. He was the only one elected by a unanimous vote. It is often said of him that he was "first in war, first in peace, and first in the hearts of his countrymen." Washington led comparatively untrained and ill-equipped American soldiers to victory over the well-trained British in the Revolutionary War. As soon as the Constitution was ratified, he was chosen to be President.

Many of the generals who had fought under Washington did not believe that the 13 colonies could cooperate to form a single country without the strong leadership of a king. They approached him, saying that they would support him as King George I of the United States. Washington was dismayed at the idea and asked the generals to promise never to mention it again. He served two terms as President and refused a third term, retiring to his farm in Virginia. When England's King George heard that Washington had voluntarily given up the power of the presidency, he said, "If that is true, he is the greatest man in history."

**7. How does the author show that George Washington is a great man? Circle the correct answer choice.**

Ⓐ  He led untrained soldiers into battle.
Ⓑ  He was unanimously elected president.
Ⓒ  He voluntarily gave up the power of the presidency.
Ⓓ  All of the above.

Michael Jordan was the greatest basketball player of all time. When he played for the Chicago Bulls, they had one winning season after another. He scored more than 100 points in 1,108 games, won two Olympic gold medals, and was ranked #1 by ESPN Magazine. Chosen for the NBA All-Stars 1 times, Jordan was ten times the scoring champ, five times the Most Valuable Player, and six time the scoring champ of the NBA. When he began losing his hair, he shaved his head completely an started a fashion trend for other players. He was chosen to make an animated movie called "Spac Jam" with Bugs Bunny. No other player has come close to those achievements.

**8. Why did the author write this passage about Michael Jordan?**

Ⓐ   To tell about how Michael Jordan made a movie with Bugs Bunny.
Ⓑ   To show what a great basketball player Michael Jordan is.
Ⓒ   To give readers Michael Jordan's life story.
Ⓓ   To tell people what it is like to be a famous basketball player.

Most of the planets in our solar system have moons. Saturn has the most, with eighteen moons. Jup ter has sixteen; Uranus has fifteen. Earth has only one, but our moon has a big influence on the live of humans on earth. In ancient times, people believed that moonlight could affect people's brain: The Latin word for the moon was Luna. Words like "lunatic" and "looney" come from that idea. Man people still believe that more babies are born and more people die when the moon is full. Scientifi studies that have been done to see whether the numbers of births and deaths actually increase whe there is a full moon show that there is no increase. The gravitational pull of the moon affects the tide in the ocean, but does not seem to affect the births and deaths of people. Does the full moon caus people to fall in love? That's another question!

**9. What point of view is the story above told from?**

Ⓐ   First person
Ⓑ   Second person
Ⓒ   Third person
Ⓓ   Fourth person

# Chapter 3

## Lesson 7: Evaluating Arguments in Text

### Fast Food Industry Statistics[1]

The number of fast food establishments in the United States peaked in 2007 at almost 218,000 units and, as the industry recovered from the global recession, this number was soon exceeded in 2010. By 2018, the number was forecasted to reach 247,191.[1]

Around 17 percent of fast food U.S. consumers dine out at quick-service restaurants at least once a month and approximately 20 percent visit them at least once a week. According to the World Health Organization, it is the unregulated frequency of such visits that is causing obesity and its related health problems in the United States. Many of the leading fast-food brands in the U.S. specialize in high-calorie foods, such as burgers, pizza and fried chicken.[1]

|  |  |  |  |
|---|---|---|---|
| **Revenue-Fast Food Restaurants 2002-2020 (Billions of dollars)** | **Number of Fast Food Restaurants 2004-2018 (In thousands)** | **Consumers' Frequency of Eating at Fast Food Establishments 2013 vs. 2014** | **Satisfaction Index Scores 2006-2017** |
| This graph shows the revenue growth of quick service restaurants in the United States from 2003 to 2014. with a forecast to 2020. | | Column 1: daily <br> Column 2: weekly <br> Column 3: monthly <br> Column 4: never | This statistic shows the American customer satisfaction index scores for limited service restaurant chains in the United States from 2006 to 2017. In 2017, the ACSI score for all limited service restaurants in the U.S. was 79. |

[1] © Statista 2017

*Let us understand the concept with an example.*

### Fast Food and Your Health

In the United States population, 30% of adults and 17% of children are obese, according to the American Heart Association. And by 2020, 83% of men and 72% of women are expected to be overweight or obese, according to research presented to the Heart Association's scientific meeting in 2011.

Food known as "fast food" served at "fast food restaurants" is a major cause, among other causes.

Fast food is unhealthy; it leads to obesity and disease, but the convenience and addictiveness of it contributes to the laziness of the general population. Most people eat fast food because they lack time to prepare a more nutritious meal. It seems as though there is a fast-food restaurant on every corner, open from early morning till late evening and offering breakfast, lunch and dinner. Fast food is addictive because it is cheap, easily accessible and tastes so good.[1]

How does fast food measure up nutritionally? The general population overlooks the fact that eating nothing but (or mostly) greasy "fast foods" will contribute to weight gain, not to mention other health related issues like clogged arteries and digestion problems. Most fast food, including drinks and sides, are loaded with carbohydrates with little or no fiber. In the digestive system, carbohydrates are released as sugar, increasing a person's blood sugar, not to mention the sugar added to some fast foods. Salt is another ingredient used in preparing fast food; salt can elevate blood pressure and place stress on the heart and cardiovascular system. Excess calories can contribute to weight gain and increase the possibility of respiratory problems such as asthma.[1]

What can people do about reducing their obesity? Control the intake of carbohydrates. Eat less processed foods, less refined grains and bread and more vegetables. Add lean protein to every meal and snack along with moderate amounts of healthy fats.

Is everything about the fast food served in fast food restaurants bad for you? "The truth is, fast food doesn't always mean 'bad for you,'" said Linda Van Horn, professor of preventive medicine at Northwestern University. "You just have to be selective, both about the choice of restaurant and the choices you make when you get there," Van Horn said. "Some, but not all, fast food restaurants have grilled chicken, salads, low-fat milk, fruit and even oatmeal choices for breakfast. Figure out which restaurants offer such options and try to frequent those more often. Consumer behavior strongly influences what restaurants choose to serve, so if you want healthier choices, choose them and let it be known. Even if you're in good heart health, try to avoid poor food choices, especially the obvious culprits that are deep fried, swimming in cream or butter, showered in salt or glittering with sugar. Even a salad that may seem healthy is just a few dollops of fatty dressing away from being bad for your heart. A salad loaded with bacon, salty high-fat dressing and cheeses can have more calories than a hamburger or piece of thin-crust pizza," Van Horn said.[2]

Footnotes:
[1] The Effects of Fast Food on the Body, by Anne Pietrangelo and Elea Carey and Kimberly Holland Healthline Media.
[2] Eating Fast Food, by Linda Van Horn, http://www.heart.org/HEARTORG, ©American Heart Association 2017

Your assignment: Integrate the information from the two articles above to develop an coherent understanding of the issues I

**This is what you might write.**

Fast food has become very popular in the United States in recent years. The number of fast food restaurants is in the thousands and the revenue from fast food sales is in the billions of dollars. One survey of fast foot restaurant patrons showed an average satisfaction index of 79 out of 100.

Why has it become so popular? One source states: "Most people eat fast food because they lack time to prepare a more nutritious meal. It seems as though there is a fast-food restaurant on every corner, open from early morning till late evening and offering breakfast, lunch and dinner. Fast food is addictive because it is cheap, easily accessible and tastes so good." But there are serious nutritional downsides to eating most fast food offerings. Some of these are: increase in blood sugar, elevated levels of sodium that can elevate blood pressure, clogged arteries, and excess calories that result in weight gain and respiratory problems like asthma.

Is it possible for people to make healthier choices about fast food? One source says it is, and gives this advice: "You just have to be selective, both about the choice of restaurant and the choices you make when you get there," Van Horn said. "Some, but not all, fast food restaurants have grilled chicken, salads, low-fat milk, fruit and even oatmeal choices for breakfast. Figure out which restaurants offer such options and try to frequent those more often." She adds: "…avoid poor food choices, especially the obvious culprits that are deep fried, swimming in cream or butter, showered in salt or glittering with sugar. Even a salad that may seem healthy is just a few dollops of fatty dressing away from being bad for your heart. A salad loaded with bacon, salty high-fat dressing and cheeses can have more calories than a hamburger or piece of thin-crust pizza."

**You can scan the QR code given below or use the url to access additional EdSearch resources including videos and mobile apps related to *Evaluating Arguments in Text*.**

 **Evaluating Arguments in Text**

| URL | QR Code |
|---|---|
| http://www.lumoslearning.com/a/ri68 |  |

Michael Jordan was the greatest basketball player of all time. He scored more than 10 points in 1,108 games, won two Olympic gold medals, and was ranked #1 by ESPN Magazine. Chosen for the NBA All-Stars 14 times, Jordan was ten times the scoring champ, five times the Most Valuable Player, and six times the scoring champ of the NBA. No other player has come close to those achievements.

**1. Identify the central idea – the claim – in the above persuasive paragraph.** _____

Ⓐ  Jordan was six times the 'scoring champ' for NBA.
Ⓑ  Jordan was chosen for the NBA All-Stars 14 times.
Ⓒ  Jordan was the greatest basketball player.
Ⓓ  Jordan was a basketball player.

Michael Jordan was the greatest basketball player of all time. When he played for the Chicago Bulls, they had one winning season after another. When he began losing his hair, he shaved his head completely and started a fashion trend for other players. He was chosen to make an animated movie called "Space Jam" with Bugs Bunny. There are many good players, but Michael Jordan will always be my favorite.

**2. The claim: Jordan was the greatest basketball player.**
**Detail to support this claim include:_____.**

Ⓐ  He was the best player on the team.
Ⓑ  When he began losing his hair, he shaved his head completely and started a fashion trend for other players.
Ⓒ  He was chosen to make an animated movie called "Space Jam" with Bugs Bunny.
Ⓓ  When he played for the Chicago Bulls, they had one winning season after another.

Life in the city is always exciting. There are more than a million people in the city where I live. There are street fairs and sidewalk vendors downtown. Most days, people are going about their daily business, just working. In that way, a big city is no different from a small town. But, in the city, there are many more concerts, lectures, theatrical performances, and other kinds of entertainment. Most of those things are expensive, and I can't afford to go. Because of the curfew, young people aren't allowed on the streets at night, and I usually have a lot of homework.

**3. Why would I like to live in a city?**

**Select the answer with the best arguments to support the above sentence:**

Ⓐ  1. City life is always exciting.
   2. There are one million people living in the city.
Ⓑ  1. There are street fairs and sidewalk vendors.
   2. There are concerts and all kinds of entertainment.
Ⓒ  1. Young people aren't allowed on the streets at night.
   2. I have a lot of homework.
Ⓓ  1. Most of the things are expensive.
   2. I can't afford to go to these exciting places.

**4. Why can't young people enjoy city life?**

**Select the answer with the best arguments to support the above sentence:**

Ⓐ  1. City life is always exciting.
   2. Too many people live in the city.
Ⓑ  1. There are street fairs and sidewalk vendors.
   2. There are concerts and all kinds of entertainment.
Ⓒ  1. There's a curfew for young people at night.
   2. Young people have no time due to too much homework.
Ⓓ  1. People go about their daily work.
   2. A big city is actually no different from a small town.


Fast food is unhealthy; it leads to obesity and disease, but the convenience and addictiveness of it contribute to the laziness of the general population. Most people eat fast food because they lack time to prepare a more nutritious meal. It seems as though there is fast food restaurant on every street corner. The general population overlooks the fact that eating nothing but these greasy foods will contribute to weight gain. Fast food is addictive because it is easily accessible and tastes so good.

**5. In the above passage, which sentence supports the argument that fast food contributes to unhealthy weight gain?**

Ⓐ  Most people eat fast food because they lack time to prepare a more nutritious meal.
Ⓑ  It seems as though there is a fast-food restaurant on every street corner.
Ⓒ  The general population overlooks the fact that eating nothing but these greasy foods will cause you to gain weight.
Ⓓ  Fast food is addictive for the convenience of it.

Kickboxing is a great form of exercise. This type of exercise tones your entire body. Punching a bag helps you gain strength and muscle in your arms. You also use the bag to do different types of kicks, thus strengthening your legs as well. Kickboxing is a total body workout that everyone should try.

**6. The claim: Kickboxing is a great form of exercise.**
   **Select the answer that most completely supports the claim:_____**

   Ⓐ  This exercise routine allows you to use a punching bag.
   Ⓑ  This exercise strengthens your muscles.
   Ⓒ  This type of exercise tones your entire body.
   Ⓓ  Kickboxing is the new trend in exercise routines.

Electric cars are a new, innovative type of car that help the environment. They use little to no gas, there by keeping pollutants out of the air. They may be a little more expensive than the average car, but you will make that money back in savings on gas. The electric car is now being made by almost all car companies.

**7. The claim: Electric cars are a new, innovative type of car.**
   **Detail to support the claim include: _____**

   Ⓐ  Electric cars are a great way to help the environment.
   Ⓑ  Electric cars are only a few years old.
   Ⓒ  Electric cars are expensive.
   Ⓓ  Most companies are now making electric cars.

Running a marathon is a great accomplishment. Training for a marathon takes months. First, you have to start running short distances, and increase the distance you run each week. During your training, you will eventually start running 20 miles at a time. A full marathon is 26.2 miles and very hard for people to finish. With a little time, training and hard work, anyone can run a marathon. Completing the marathon is a great accomplishment because it shows excellent dedication and athletic ability.

**8. Identify the claim in this passage.**

   Ⓐ  Running a marathon requires you to train a lot.
   Ⓑ  Running a marathon is a great accomplishment.
   Ⓒ  Running requires excellent dedication.
   Ⓓ  Not many people are able to complete a marathon.

Smartphones are the newest innovative technology out there. On the smartphone you can video chat with your friends or family members to keep in touch. Smartphones also are a great way to stay organized and keep your life on track. Smartphones are an easy way to search the internet when you are out and need to find something quickly. They allow you to access tons of information.

**9. Which sentence is the claim of the passage?**

Horses are used for many different types of activities. Horses can be used to pull carts. They are also used for riding English style in which the rider can jump and show them. Horses can also be used for riding Western style in which riders can herd and rope cattle and go on trail rides. An English style rider can also perform dressage, which is a highly precise series of movements involving the rider and the horse.

**10. Identify the claim in this paragraph.**

Ⓐ  Dressage is the most intricate form of horse training.
Ⓑ  Horses can be used for many different activities.
Ⓒ  Horses can be ridden English style.
Ⓓ  Horses can be ridden Western style.

Michael Phelps is the most decorated American athlete in Olympic history. Michael Phelps has won more gold medals in his swimming career than any other American Olympian. He also has won the most gold medals in one Olympic game. Michael Phelps will become the most decorated Olympian world wide if he wins during the London 2012 summer Olympics.

**11. Identify the claim in this paragraph.**

## Chapter 3

## Lesson 8: Compare/Contrast One Author's Presentation with Another

*Let us understand the concept with an example.*

### Global Warming

For many years, scientists have been studying the effects of temperature on living organisms o
planet Earth. In the last few years, there has been an increase in the Earth's atmospheric and ocean
temperatures, which has been called global warming. Global warming has been recognized as
very important environmental phenomenon that can have dramatic and devastating effects on th
environment of planet Earth.

Scientists in one group, we'll call it Group A, believe the theory that global warming is caused by th
increase in certain gases (such as carbon dioxide) in the atmosphere that occurs when warmth fror
the sun is trapped in the Earth's atmosphere by a layer of gases (such as carbon dioxide) and wate
vapor. They refer to this as the "greenhouse effect."  This group believes that human activities, suc
as manufacturing, deforestation and pollution are the primary contributors to the greenhouse effec

*Group A provides the following key details to support their theory:*

An IPCC (United Nations' Intergovernmental Panel on Climate Change) report, based on the work o
some 2,500 scientists in more than 130 countries, concluded that humans have caused all or most o
the current planetary warming. Human-caused global warming is often called anthropogenic climat
change. Industrialization, deforestation, and pollution have greatly increased atmospheric concentra
tions of water vapor, carbon dioxide, methane, and nitrous oxide, all greenhouse gases that help tra
heat near Earth's surface. Humans are pouring carbon dioxide into the atmosphere much faster tha
plants and oceans can absorb it.

Also, 97% of the climate scientists surveyed believe "global average temperatures have increasec
during the past century, and 97% think human activity is a significant contributing factor in changin
mean global temperatures.

Scientists in another group, we'll call it Group B, believe the theory that global warming is not just
recent phenomenon, but is a natural phenomenon that has been occurring for thousands of years o
part of a cycle of warming and cooling of the earth's atmosphere, and that human activity is only
minor contributor.

*Group B provides the following key details to support their theory:*

First, 31,000 scientists reject global warming and say there is "no convincing evidence" that humans can or will cause global warming. This claim originates from an organization which published an online  petition that they claim 31,000 scientists have signed.

Second, they mention that some experts point out that natural cycles in the Earth's orbit can alter the planet's exposure to sunlight, which may explain the current trend. Earth has indeed experienced warming and cooling cycles roughly every hundred thousand years due to these orbital shifts, but such changes have occurred over the span of several centuries.

Third, they claim that in 2009, hackers unearthed hundreds of emails stored at a university that exposed private conversations among some top-level climate scientists discussing whether certain data that did not support Group A's theory should be released to the public (or held and not released). The email exchanges also refer to statistical tricks used to illustrate climate change trends, according to a report in one major newspaper. Climate change skeptics have heralded the emails as an attempt to fool the public into accepting Group A's theory.

*Your assignment: Compare and contrast the positions of Group A and Group B based on the Global Warming article.*

**This is what you might write.**

Group A and Group B both agree that global warming is occurring, but beyond that, they do not agree.

Group A believes that "global warming is caused by the increase of certain gases (such as carbon dioxide) in the atmosphere that occurs when warmth from the sun is trapped in the Earth's atmosphere by a layer of gases (such as carbon dioxide) and water vapor." They cite studies measuring the increase of carbon dioxide and other pollutant gases in the atmosphere over a period of years. They cite one study within the United Nations that supports the theory "that human activities, such as manufacturing, deforestation and pollution are the primary contributors to the greenhouse effect." As a result of their conclusions, there has been an increased awareness worldwide of the negative effects of global warming, and many governmental and private organizations have spent time and money investigating ways to reduce global emissions. I have personally read literature and seen TV programs promoting the views of Group A.

Group B believes that "global warming is not just a recent phenomenon, but is a natural phenomenon that has been occurring for thousands of years as part of a cycle of warming and cooling of the earth's atmosphere, and that human activity is only a minor contributor." The article lists three reasons in support of their theory.

Although it does not say this in the article, I have seen evidence that Group A seeks to raise awareness of the dangers of global warming and to participate in efforts to control it through legal agreements restricting the human activities they believe contribute to it. I also have seen evidence that Group B is working to oppose the efforts of Group A to combat global warming. They view it as an unnecessary expenditure of time and money, since natural phenomena will cause a change to global warming naturally, without human intervention.

**You can scan the QR code given below or use the url to access additional EdSearch resources including videos and mobile apps related to *Compare/Contrast One Author's Presentation with Another.***

## Compare/Contrast One Author's Presentation with Another

| URL | QR Code |
|---|---|
| http://www.lumoslearning.com/a/ri66 |  |

"Peace cannot be achieved through violence, it can only be attained through understanding." - Ralph Waldo Emerson

"Peace cannot be kept by force; it can only be achieved by understanding." - Albert Einstein

## 1. What do both of these individuals say about peace?

Ⓐ  You can only have peace by fighting.
Ⓑ  You can only have peace through understanding.
Ⓒ  You can only have peace when everyone gets along.
Ⓓ  Peace is all around us.

"Music is a world within itself, with a language we all understand." - Stevie Wonder

"Without music, life would be a mistake." - Fredrich Nietzsche

## 2. What is similar about these two quotations?

Ⓐ  Both talk about languages.
Ⓑ  Both talk about life.
Ⓒ  Both talk about music.
Ⓓ  They have nothing similar.

## 3. Which one of the answers below is a great way to visually compare and contrast information?

Ⓐ  Venn Diagram
Ⓑ  Chart
Ⓒ  Graph
Ⓓ  All of the above

## 4. To compare and contrast means _____

Ⓐ  Explain the details about two things
Ⓑ  Explain how two things are different
Ⓒ  Explain how two things are alike
Ⓓ  Explain how two things are alike and different

## 5. Lakes and ponds are similar because _____.

Ⓐ  They are saltwater
Ⓑ  You can fish in them
Ⓒ  You can jet ski in them
Ⓓ  You can sail in them

**6. Snowfall and rainfall are similar. Which of the following is true with both of these?**

   Ⓐ  Wet drops that accumulate on the ground ~~and~~ *can* cause hazardous driving conditions
   Ⓑ  Large drops that are white and clear
   Ⓒ  Wet drops that turn to ice
   Ⓓ  Wet drops that disappear when they touch the ground

**Read the quotations and then answer the question that follows.**

1. "For every disciplined effort there is a multiple reward." - Jim Rohn

2. "Genius is one percent inspiration and ninety-nine percent perspiration." - Thomas Alva Edison

**7. Both Edison and Rohn are talking about the benefit of _____.**

   Ⓐ  genius
   Ⓑ  reward
   Ⓒ  effort
   Ⓓ  inspiration

"Friendship is not something you learn in school.  But if you haven't learned the meaning of friend ship, you really haven't learned anything." - Muhammad Ali

"If you live to be 100, I hope to live to be 100 minus 1 day, so I never have to live without you. - Winnie the Pooh

**8. What do both of these quotations have in common?**

   Ⓐ  They are both about living life.
   Ⓑ  They are both about friendship.
   Ⓒ  They are both about learning.
   Ⓓ  They have nothing in common

**Read the quotations and then answer the question that follows.**

"Education is the most powerful weapon which you can use to change the world."  Nelson Mandela

"Be the change you wish to see in the world."  Gandhi

**9. Both of these quotations talk about changing the world.  What two contrasting things do they say makes change in the world?**

Ⓐ  Education, yourself
Ⓑ  Weapons, yourself
Ⓒ  Yourself, man
Ⓓ  Education; weapons

**10. The desert is hot and dry whereas the _____ are cold and icy.**

Ⓐ  Mountains
Ⓑ  Forests
Ⓒ  Tropical islands
Ⓓ  Polar regions

If your actions inspire others to dream more, learn more, do more and become more, you are a leader. - John Quincy Adams

The key to successful leadership today is influence, not authority.- Kenneth Blanchard

**11. The above statements tells us that they are talking about _____.**

**12. Fill in the blank**
    **The desert is hot and dry whereas the _____ are cold and icy.**

# End of Reading: Informational Text

# Answer Key and
# Detailed Explanations

## Chapter 3
## Reading: Informational Text

# Lesson 1: Cite Textual Evidence

| Question No. | Answer | Detailed Explanations |
|---|---|---|
| 1 | A | The text specifically states that an empty gallery had 42,000 germs but when filled with people, that same gallery had nearly 5,000,000 germs. One can then conclude that a crowded space will hold more germs. The correct answer is A. |
| 2 | D | While Louis Pasteur discovered germs there is no evidence in the story to support that he liked counting germs.  Yes, germs are too small to be seen with the naked eye but they can be seen using powerful microscopes.  Even though people do carry germs, the best concluding statement from this passage would be that there are fewer germs in fresh air.  The correct answer is D. |
| 3 | D | Throughout the passage, each of the options is pointed out as something significant George Washington did in order to make him a great man.  One can draw the conclusion that each factor makes him a great man. |
| 4 | C | The text implies that George Washington was not interested in being powerful; therefore Answer B would not be a correct choice. There is no evidence within the text that either supports or disputes that George Washington was a kind man. While his actions certainly showed that he was a smart man, the fact that George Washington was a strong leader is implied in how he led his army as well as knowing when it was his time to share the power by leaving office |
| 5 | B | At the beginning of the passage, the text not only states that George Washington is the most popular president but also specifically states that he was elected by a unanimous vote which means that everyone voted for him thus giving him the popular vote. |
| 6 | B | In the last paragraph, the passage states that Vanderbilt regretted dismissing Westinghouse's idea of an air brake.  As a result, one can conclude that Vanderbilt regretted not taking the time to hear about Westinghouse's invention.  The correct answer is B. |
| 7 | A | While it is true that Michael Jordan did shave his head, it does not support the idea that he is the greatest basketball player of all time; whereas all the other statements do support this idea.  The correct answer is A. |

| Question No. | Answer | Detailed Explanations |
|:---:|:---:|---|
| 8 | B | While Michael Jordan did star in a movie with Bugs Bunny, this is not the most significant part of the passage. Yes, it tells a little about Michael Jordan's life but it is not his life story, it is merely highlights of his career as a famous basketball player. Since the passage tells primarily about Michael Jordan as a basketball player and all he has accomplished, it can be concluded that the author wrote the passage to show what a great basketball player he is. The correct answer is B |
| 9 | D | The passage specifically states that our moon is thought to influence the lives of humans. Therefore, the correct answer is D. |
| 10 | A | There is no evidence in the passage which shows that either our moon is less powerful because we only have one or that our moon is bigger than Jupiter's. The text does suggest that people believe the moon causes crazy things to happen like more births, deaths, and people falling in love but there is no proof these things happen. The only thing the passage says for sure, is that people do believe that "looney" things happen and since looney is a synonym for crazy, the correct answer is A. |
| 11 | D | It says in the text that the nervous system tells the body what to do. It other words, it controls the body. |

# Lesson 2: Central Idea of Text

| Question No. | Answer | Detailed Explanations |
|---|---|---|
| 1 Part A | B | The central idea is that mountain men liked Shakespeare, even if they could not read. Sentence six exemplifies this idea the most. |
| 1 Part B | D | More men had Shakespeare than the Bible, and they memorized Shakespeare. That shows how much they loved it. |
| 2 | A | The fact that mountain men carried books around for years does not directly prove that they liked Shakespeare best. |
| 3 | B | The only answer that is a clear central idea is answer choice B. Option C is a supporting detail. Options A and D are not mentioned. |
| 4 | B | Central ideas are general. If a statement is too specific, then it might be a supporting detail and not the central idea. |
| 5 | D | The central idea of a passage is supported by details that follow it. That's why the answer is D. |
| 6 | A | If you decided on A. Sentences #9 and #10 help the reader remember the definition of homograph and homophone, you made the best choice.

The purpose of those details is to help the reader remember the difference between the two terms: homophone and homograph. |
| 7 | A | If you looked first at Sentences #1 and #10, you were checking wisely. The central idea of a paragraph is often the first or the last sentence. In this case, Sentence #10 is a supporting detail, and Sentence #1 is the central idea. |
| 8 | A | If you looked first at Sentence #3 and then chose A, you made the right decision. Supporting details generally follow the idea they're supporting. |
| 9 | B | If you selected B, Sentence #6, you made the right choice. The supporting details often follow immediately the sentence they support. |
| 10 Part A | B | Although all of the things above are mentioned, the paragraph is mainly about the germs. |
| 10 Part B | D | All of the things above are mentioned in the first paragraph, so the correct answer is D. |
| 11 | | The entire area is about washing clothes |

# Lesson 3: Analyze how People, Events or Ideas are Presented in Text

| Question No. | Answer | Detailed Explanations |
|---|---|---|
| 1 | B | Answer choices A, C, and D present minor details related to the bigger, overall topic that germs are everywhere. The correct answer is B. |
| 2 | C | Answer choice C is the only answer that is not even presented in the story; therefore it is not a supporting detail. The correct answer is C. |
| 3 | D | Answers A and B both provide supporting details. Answer choice C is a misinterpretation of the text. Answer choice D presents what the passage is about – George Washington was a great general and president. |
| 4 | C | The text implies that George Washington was not interested in being powerful; therefore Answer B would not be a correct choice. There is no evidence within the text that either supports or disputes that George Washington was a kind man. While his actions certainly showed that he was a smart man, the fact that George Washington was a strong leader is implied in how he led his army as well as knew when it was his time to share the power by leaving office. |
| 5 | A | The only answer choice which completely identifies who Michael Jordan is and why is answer choice A. This would make the best, broad introductory sentence. |
| 6 | D | Both answer choices A and B support the central idea of the passage that Michael Jordan is a great basketball player. Answer choice C does not support the central idea. The correct answer choice is D. |
| 7 | D | While the passage does talk about the railroads, Vanderbilt, and air brakes, it is actually about George Westinghouse's invention of the air brake. The correct answer is D. |
| 8 | B | Even though Vanderbilt felt Westinghouse was a fool, Westinghouse kept trying. The passage specifically states that Westinghouse went on to try another railroad that listened to his ideas and tested his air brake. The correct answer is B. |
| 9 | C | While the fact that Westinghouse invented something very important, the air brake, shows that he is smart and he did demonstrate that he is courteous in his interactions with Vanderbilt, he is best described as determined because he did not give up. Only Vanderbilt described Westinghouse as foolish. The correct answer is C. |

| Question No. | Answer | Detailed Explanations |
|---|---|---|
| 10 | A | While each of the answer choices are true, only answer choice A illustrates how books were important to mountain men and that was because they were hard to get. |
| 11 | B | The author specifically states that certain parts of clothing or dress need special attention or care. The author then goes on to support this idea. The correct answer choice is B. |

# Lesson 4: Determine Technical Meanings

| Question No. | Answer | Detailed Explanations |
|---|---|---|
| 1 | A | Answer A is correct because synonyms will basically have the same definition as the original word they are representing. |
| 2 | D | The words will have completely opposite meanings, so the answer is D. |
| 3 | C | homophone - same pronunciation, spelled differently, different meanings.<br>homonyms - same spelling, different meaning.<br>homographs - spelled the same, not necessarily pronounced the same, and different meaning<br>homo-word - not found in grammar,<br><br>minute - time is pronounced with a short vowel i and the u sounds like a short vowel i.<br>minute - small is pronounced with a long vowel i and a long vowel u.<br>Hence, answer choice C is correct. These are homographs. |
| 4 | D | Answer choice D is correct because those two words are complete opposites. |
| 5 | A | Answer choice A contains the synonym. The other answer choices are antonyms. |
| 6 | D | Answer choice D is the only one that gives words with opposite meanings, or antonyms. |
| 7 | C | Worms and germs are an almost perfect rhyme, so the answer is C. |
| 8 | B | That is the exact definition of a homonym, so the answer is B. |
| 9 | C | Answer choice C is correct because that is the exact definition of a homophone. |
| 10 | D | Answer choices A and B both have words that sound the same but are spelled differently and have different meanings. For that reason, the correct answer is D. |
| 11 Part A | B | That is the technical definition of a synonym, so the answer is B. |
| 11 Part B | A | Answer choice A is correct because that is the definition of an antonym. |

# Lesson 5: Structure of Text

| Question No. | Answer | Detailed Explanations |
|---|---|---|
| 1 | B | If you chose B, the missing sentence should be second, you made the best choice. Although it says "Start," you cannot start until you know what you are starting to do, so the missing sentence should not be first. You should select the freshest bread before you take the pieces of it, so the missing sentence should not be third, and it would not make sense in the fourth position. |
| 2 | C | If you chose C, the missing sentence should be third, you picked the right answer. The phrase, "continue the aerobic training" lets you know that aerobic training had to have already begun at some point, and it is mentioned in the second sentence. |
| 3 | B | If you chose B, the missing sentence should be second, you picked the best response. The definition of potpourri should come before it is mentioned that they were originally made in France, and that the flowers and leaves sat for months. |
| 4 | B | If you chose B, you made the right decision. Only option B gives the arrangement that would be a good sequence for the sentences. |
| 5 | A | If you picked A, you made the best choice. If the paragraph doesn't begin with sentence 4, the reader will not know what the paragraph is talking about, and sentence 4 is only offered once as the first choice. |
| 6 | A | If you put the paragraph in reverse order, it reads perfectly. That is why A is the correct answer. |
| 7 | C | This piece gives information, so answer choice C is correct. |
| 8 | A | If the paper were written by Westinghouse and about his experience, then it would be a personal narrative. |
| 9 | D | All of the above mentioned things are part of an essay. Answer choice D is correct. |
| 10 | D | All of these things are part of a business letter. |
| 11 | D | The salutation is the beginning of the letter where you say "Dear Sir or Madam". |
| 12 | C | Although there will be description of some kind, there will be more in the narrative and the descriptive writing about a winter day will have the most. |

# Lesson 6: Determine Author's Point of View

| Question No. | Answer | Detailed Explanations |
| --- | --- | --- |
| 1 | C | The passage is trying to persuade the reader as to why dogs are better pets than cats. The correct answer is C. |
| 2 | A | The passage is giving information on how words are added to or deleted from the dictionary. The correct answer is A. |
| 3 Part A | B | The passage is explaining how to make a peanut butter and jelly sandwich. The correct answer is B. |
| 3 Part B | B | The passage is giving directions with no narrator, therefore it is told from second person point of view. |
| 4 | A | The passage is giving information about germs. The correct answer is A. |
| 5 | C | While the passage says that football is an exciting sport and that there is never a dull moment, the author does not use persuasive language aimed at convincing the reader. Also, the passage does not tell a story. It does, however, tell about what happens at a game. The correct answer is C. |
| 6 | A | The passage ends by saying "you should eat vegetables at least 3 meals a day." It also gives information to backup why this is important. Therefore, the passage is trying to convince readers to eat more vegetables. The correct answer is A. |
| 7 | D | Throughout the passage, each of the options is pointed out as something significant George Washington did in order to make him a great man. One can draw the conclusion that each factor makes him a great man. |
| 8 | B | While Michael Jordan did star in a movie with Bugs Bunny, this is not the most significant part of the passage. Yes, it tells a little about Michael Jordan's life but it is not his life story, it is merely highlights of his career as a famous basketball player. Since the passage tells primarily about Michael Jordan as a basketball player and all he has accomplished, it can be concluded that the author wrote the passage to show what a great basketball player he is. The correct answer is B. |
| 9 | C | Since the passage is providing factual information, it is told from third person point of view. |

# Lesson 7: Evaluating Arguments in Text

| Question No. | Answer | Detailed Explanations |
|---|---|---|
| 1 | C | All of the evidence in the passage points to the fact that Jordan was a truly great basketball player. That is why the central idea can be found in answer choice C. |
| 2 | D | It was not mentioned in the passage that he was the best player on the team. The only detail that supports the main idea is D, he contributed to many of the Bulls' wins. |
| 3 | B | Answer choice B contains two positive things about living in the city. Those are the two sentences that support why the author likes living in the city. |
| 4 | C | Answer choice C gives two reasons why young people can't enjoy city life. The other answers do not contain relevant arguments. |
| 5 | C | Answer choice C is the only one that mentions gaining weight, and the other answers do not support the argument listed above. |
| 6 | C | Answer choice C is the one that most completely goes with the claim that kickboxing is a great form of exercise. Every exercise strengthens the muscles, and it does not mention in the article anything about it being a new trend. It does mention a punching bag, but that is only one part of kickboxing. |
| 7 | A | Although all of the answers contain true statements, only answer choice A supports the claim that the cars are innovative in that they are good for the environment. |
| 8 | B | The claim, or controlling idea, is usually at the beginning of the paragraph. That is true in this case. The answer is B because that's what the first sentence says. |
| 9 | | The opening sentence is the claim, or the controlling idea i.e., Smartphones are the newest innovative technology out there. |
| 10 | B | The claim in this paragraph is the central idea, or controlling idea. It's what the author is trying to convince you of. Answer choice B contains the claim of this passage. |
| 11 | | The passage doesn't say anything about him having the most silver medals, but the claim in the paragraph is that he is the most decorated Olympic athlete (which means he has the most medals.) |

# Lesson 8: Compare/Contrast One Author's Presentation with Another

| Question No. | Answer | Detailed Explanations |
| --- | --- | --- |
| 1 | B | Both men are talking about how peace can only be attained through non-violence and understanding. The correct answer is B. |
| 2 | C | Both quotations, while having a different message, speak about the importance and value of music. The correct answer choice is C. |
| 3 | D | You can use all of the above to effectively compare and contrast. |
| 4 | D | Comparing is seeing how things are alike and contrasting is seeing how they are different. For that reason, the answer is D. |
| 5 | B | Ponds are not big enough to jet ski or sail in, and ponds and lakes are fresh water bodies of water. The only answer that is true is B. |
| 6 | A | Answer choice A is the only one that describes both rain and snow. The other answers only describe one, either rain or snow. |
| 7 | C | Both quotes are about effort, so the correct answer is C. |
| 8 | B | Both of these quotes are about friendship even if it is not specifically stated. The correct answer is B. |
| 9 | A | While both quotes talk about changing the world, the first quote stresses that education leads to change whereas the second quote suggests that you yourself create change. The correct answer is A. |
| 10 | D | Polar regions are the only logical answer because they are cold and icy. The correct answer is D. |
| 11 | leadership | Both quotes mention leadership |
| 12 | Polar regions | Polar regions are the only logical answer because they are cold and icy. |

# Chapter 4 - Language

The objective of the Language standards is to ensure that the student is able to accurately use grade appropriate general academic and domain specific words and phrases related to Grade 6.

To help students master the necessary skills, we encourage the student to go through the resources available online on EdSearch to gain an in depth understanding of these concepts. The EdSearch page for each lesson can be accessed with the help of the url or the QR code provided.

Name: _____ Date: _____

## Chapter 4

## Lesson 1: Correct subject-verb agreement

You can scan the QR code given below or use the url to access additional EdSearch resources including videos and mobile apps related to *Correct subject-verb agreement.*

 **Correct subject-verb agreement**

| URL | QR Code |
|---|---|
| http://www.lumoslearning.com/a/l61 |  |

. **Correct the following sentence to show subject-verb agreement.**

Tracy and Gary likes to solve puzzles.

- Ⓐ Tracy and Gary likes to solve puzzles.
- Ⓑ Tracy and Gary like to solve puzzles.
- Ⓒ Tracy and Gary like to solves puzzle.
- Ⓓ Tracy likes to solve puzzle.

. **Correct the following sentence to show subject-verb agreement.**

All of the students competes for the prizes.

- Ⓐ All of the student competes for the prizes.
- Ⓑ All of the students compete for the prizes.
- Ⓒ The students competes for the prizes.
- Ⓓ None of the above

. **Correct the following sentence to show subject-verb agreement.**

Many people considers tea a stimulant.

- Ⓐ Many a people considers tea a stimulant.
- Ⓑ Many people consider tea a stimulant.
- Ⓒ Many peoples consider tea a stimulant.
- Ⓓ The above sentence needs no correction.

. **Correct the verb to show correct subject-verb agreement.**

The enemies plots revenge and won the battle this time.

- Ⓐ The enemy plot revenge and win the battle this time.
- Ⓑ The enemy plot revenge and will win the battle this time.
- Ⓒ The enemy will plot revenge and will won the battle this time.
- Ⓓ The enemies plot revenge and win the battle this time.

. **Correct the following sentence to make it correct.**

Sally finish her project earlier than the others.

- Ⓐ Sally finish her projects earlier than the others.
- Ⓑ Sally finished her project earlier than the others.
- Ⓒ Sally have already finish her project earlier than the others.
- Ⓓ Sally finishing her project earlier than the others.

**6. Fill in the blank with the correct word that fits in the sentence.**

Some of the votes _____ to have been miscounted.

- Ⓐ  seems
- Ⓑ  seem
- Ⓒ  will seem
- Ⓓ  shall seem

**7. Fill in the blank with the correct word that fits in the sentence.**

All of the dancers_____ to be sick.

- Ⓐ  appear
- Ⓑ  has appeared
- Ⓒ  will appear
- Ⓓ  appears

**8. Fill in the blank with the correct word that fits in the sentence.**

Parents and students _____ against the hike in tuition fee.

- Ⓐ  is
- Ⓑ  are
- Ⓒ  are being
- Ⓓ  had been

**9. Fill in the blank with the correct word that fits in the sentence.**

Either the Principal in this School or the Chief Administrator _____ to make a quick decision.

- Ⓐ  have
- Ⓑ  will
- Ⓒ  has
- Ⓓ  are

**10. Fill in the blank with the correct word that fits in the sentence.**

She seems to forget that there _____ things to be done before the expedition.

- Ⓐ  is
- Ⓑ  has
- Ⓒ  are
- Ⓓ  have

**11. Correct the following sentence to show subject-verb agreement.**

The girls' shirt is lime green.

**12. Correct the following sentence to show subject-verb agreement.**

Tony climb the tree every day after school.

**13. Correct the following sentence to show subject-verb agreement.**

The team are going to win the game.

## Chapter 4

## Lesson 2: Correct Use of Adjectives and Adverbs

You can scan the QR code given below or use the url to access additional EdSearch resources including videos and mobile apps related to *Correct Use of Adjectives and Adverbs*.

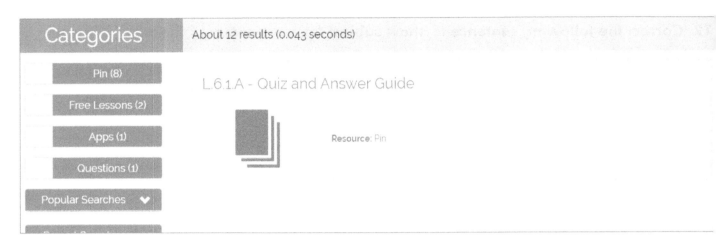

| ed Search | **Correct Use of Adjectives and Adverbs** |
|---|---|
| **URL** | **QR Code** |
| http://www.lumoslearning.com/a/l61 | |

**1. Identify the adjective in the following sentence.**

The book that I was reading had colorful pages.

- Ⓐ colorful
- Ⓑ reading
- Ⓒ pages
- Ⓓ book

**2. Identify the adjective/adjectives in the following sentence.**

Earth is the most beautiful planet in the solar system.

- Ⓐ Earth
- Ⓑ beautiful
- Ⓒ system
- Ⓓ planet

**3. Identify the adjective in this sentence.**

The frightened alien ran back into its airship.

- Ⓐ airship
- Ⓑ alien
- Ⓒ frightened
- Ⓓ ran

**4. Identify the adverb in the following sentence.**

The mother was quite unhappy to see her son leave.

- Ⓐ quite
- Ⓑ unhappy
- Ⓒ the
- Ⓓ leave

**5. Identify the adverb in the following sentence.**

The long wait made him utterly tired.

- Ⓐ long
- Ⓑ wait
- Ⓒ tired
- Ⓓ utterly

**6. Identify the adverb in the following sentence and point out the verb it modifies/describes**

My clever friend answered all the questions correctly.

- Ⓐ  adverb: clever ; verb: friend
- Ⓑ  adverb: correctly ; verb: questions
- Ⓒ  adverb: correctly ; verb: answered
- Ⓓ  adverb: clever : verb: question

**7. Identify the adverb in the following sentence.**

The girl politely asked the boy for her book back.

**8. Identify the adjective or adjectives in the following sentence.**

The polka dot umbrella protected Ted from the cold rain.

- Ⓐ  polka dot and protected
- Ⓑ  umbrella and polka dot
- Ⓒ  umbrella and rain
- Ⓓ  polka dot and cold

**9. Identify the adverb in the following sentence.**

Last night, the whole family slept soundly.

- Ⓐ  soundly
- Ⓑ  last
- Ⓒ  slept
- Ⓓ  night

**10. Identify the adverb in the following sentence.**

The computer printer hardly works.

**11. Identify the adverb in the following sentence.**

Peter is really busy.

## Chapter 4

## Lesson 3: Recognize Pronouns

You can scan the QR code given below or use the url to access additional EdSearch resources including videos and mobile apps related to *Recognize Pronouns*.

 **ed Search**

### *Recognize Pronouns*

| URL | QR Code |
|-----|---------|
| http://www.lumoslearning.com/a/l61 |  |

**1. Choose the correct pronoun to complete the sentence.**

I did it by _____.

- (A) me
- (B) myself
- (C) I
- (D) my

**2. Choose the correct pronoun to complete the sentence.**

We _____ are responsible for the decorations.

- (A) us
- (B) ourselves
- (C) themselves
- (D) myself

**3. Choose the correct pronoun to complete the sentence.**

She made up the story _____ .

- (A) himself
- (B) herself
- (C) itself
- (D) themself

**4. Choose the correct pronoun to complete the sentence.**

If a student wants to do well, _____ to get plenty of sleep.

- (A) you have
- (B) he or she has
- (C) you has
- (D) they have

**5. Choose the correct pronoun to complete the sentence.**

The best poker players can keep _____ faces from showing any reaction.

- (A) her
- (B) its
- (C) their
- (D) his

**6. Correct the following sentence to make the referent clear.**

Charlie danced with his friend Carol and Sue most of the evening. She is his girlfriend.

- Ⓐ Sue is his girlfriend.
- Ⓑ He is her friend.
- Ⓒ She is the girlfriend.
- Ⓓ Carol is his girlfriend.

**7. Correct the following sentence to make the referent clear.**

Riding without a helmet is a big risk. This is unnecessary.

- Ⓐ They are unnecessary.
- Ⓑ This risk is unnecessary.
- Ⓒ It is unnecessary.
- Ⓓ Riding is unnecessary.

**8. Correct the following sentence to make the referent clear.**

The cat ate the goldfish before I could stop the tragedy. It was terrible.

- Ⓐ They are terrible.
- Ⓑ The tragedy was terrible.
- Ⓒ The goldfish was terrible.
- Ⓓ The cat was terrible.

**9. Correct the following sentence to make the referent clear.**

Johnny is taller than Ahmed. He's grown a lot this year.

**10. Correct the following sentence to make the referent clear.**

The Sharks and the Jets were the gangs in West Side Story. They performed great dances.

- Ⓐ The gangs performed great dances.
- Ⓑ The sharks performed great dances.
- Ⓒ It performed great dances.
- Ⓓ The Jets performed great dances.

**11. Correct the following sentence to make the referent clear.**

Carrots are better than beets. They give you Vitamin A.

[ ]

**12. Correct the following sentence to make the referent clear.**

Walking and running are more aerobic than playing team sports. They are fun, too.

[ ]

## Chapter 4

## Lesson 4: Recognize and Correct Shifts in Pronoun

You can scan the QR code given below or use the url to access additional EdSearch resources including videos and mobile apps related to *Recognize and Correct Shifts in Pronoun*.

| URL | QR Code |
|-----|---------|
| **ed Search** | **Recognize and Correct Shifts in Pronoun** |
| http://www.lumoslearning.com/a/l61 |  |

**1. Fill in the blank with the correct pronoun, which best completes the following sentence?**

Each student got to choose _____ own desk.

**2. Fill in the blank with the correct pronoun, which best completes the following sentence?**

All the girls were excited to be able to wear _____ new dresses to the dance.

**3. Fill in the blank with the correct pronoun, which best completes the following sentence?**

Coach Bob was proud of the way _____ team played in the game.

**4. Which pronoun best completes the following sentence?**

Billy and _____ plan to ride our bikes to the park as soon as school is out.

Ⓐ  I
Ⓑ  me
Ⓒ  us
Ⓓ  his

**5. Which pronoun best completes the following sentence?**

Mrs. Marshall's students won the reading contest. _____ read more books than any other class in the sixth grade.

Ⓐ  Their
Ⓑ  Her
Ⓒ  They
Ⓓ  I

**6. Which pronoun best completes the following sentence?**

Johnny's friends are all on the football team with _____.

Ⓐ  her
Ⓑ  his
Ⓒ  it
Ⓓ  him

**7. Which pronoun best completes the following sentence?**

Lucy loves to have pepperoni and onions with extra cheese on _____ pizza.

- Ⓐ her
- Ⓑ their
- Ⓒ his
- Ⓓ my

**8. Which pronoun best completes the following sentence?**

_____ can't wait to go to see my Aunt Sara for the holidays.

- Ⓐ We
- Ⓑ He
- Ⓒ I
- Ⓓ They

**9. Which pronoun best completes the following sentence?**

When Tiffany went ice skating, _____ fell and twisted her ankle.

- Ⓐ she
- Ⓑ her
- Ⓒ my
- Ⓓ we

**10. Which pronoun best completes the following sentence?**

My dog loves playing catch with his ball, except _____ never brings it back.

- Ⓐ they
- Ⓑ she
- Ⓒ he
- Ⓓ I

## Chapter 4

## Lesson 5: Recognize and Correct Vague Pronouns

You can scan the QR code given below or use the url to access additional EdSearch resources including videos and mobile apps related to *Recognize and Correct Vague Pronouns*.

 **Search**     *Recognize and Correct Vague Pronouns*

| URL | QR Code |
|---|---|
| http://www.lumoslearning.com/a/l61 |  |

**1. Choose the pronoun that agrees with the antecedent in the following sentence.**

Anybody who forgets _____ homework will have detention at lunch.

Ⓐ his
Ⓑ my
Ⓒ its
Ⓓ their

**2. Choose the pronoun that agrees with the antecedent in the following sentence.**

The students made _____ own costumes for the play.

Ⓐ her
Ⓑ their
Ⓒ my
Ⓓ our

**3. Choose the pronoun that agrees with the antecedent in the following sentence.**

Gavin's dog follows _____ everywhere.

Ⓐ their
Ⓑ me
Ⓒ his
Ⓓ him

**4. Choose the pronoun that agrees with the antecedent in the following sentence.**

Emily and Nathan both love to sing so _____ are going to do a duet for the talent show.

Ⓐ they
Ⓑ he
Ⓒ she
Ⓓ their

**5. Choose the pronoun that agrees with the antecedent in the following sentence.**

The students practiced many hours in preparation for _____ concert.

Ⓐ their
Ⓑ there
Ⓒ our
Ⓓ his

5. Choose the pronoun that agrees with the antecedent in the following sentence.

Roger stayed up late to finish _____ English project.

- Ⓐ our
- Ⓑ his
- Ⓒ their
- Ⓓ my

7. Fill in the blank with the pronoun that agrees with the antecedent in the following sentence.

Mary left the cookies out on the counter so I ate _____.

8. Fill in the blank with the pronoun that agrees with the antecedent in the following sentence.

The store was having a huge sale on all _____ shoes.

9. Fill in the blank with the pronoun that agrees with the antecedent in the following sentence.

Even though Patty is packed for the trip, _____ does not feel ready to go.

10. Choose the pronoun that agrees with the antecedent in the following sentence.

Billy and Luis both forgot to bring _____ sleeping bags on the camping trip.

- Ⓐ his
- Ⓑ my
- Ⓒ our
- Ⓓ their

## Chapter 4

## Lesson 6: Recognize Variations in English

You can scan the QR code given below or use the url to access additional EdSearch resource including videos and mobile apps related to *Recognize Variations in English*.

 **Search**

### *Recognize Variations in English*

| URL | QR Code |
|-----|---------|
| http://www.lumoslearning.com/a/l61 |  |

**1. What is the correct way to write the underlined part of the following sentence?**

Yesterday my mom baked cookies and we <u>eat</u> them all.

- Ⓐ  will eat
- Ⓑ  did eat
- Ⓒ  eaten
- Ⓓ  ate

**2. What is the correct way to write the underlined part of the following sentence?**

Jenny went to the store and <u>buy</u> apples, milk, and bread.

- Ⓐ  bought
- Ⓑ  will buy
- Ⓒ  did buy
- Ⓓ  buyed

**3. What is the correct way to write the underlined part of the following sentence?**

Billy and Matt rode <u>they're</u> bikes to the park.

- Ⓐ  there
- Ⓑ  their
- Ⓒ  they
- Ⓓ  them

**4. What is the correct way to write the underlined part of the following sentence?**

My dad and I <u>builds</u> a tree house together this weekend.

- Ⓐ  will build
- Ⓑ  built
- Ⓒ  had built
- Ⓓ  build

**5. What is the correct way to write the underlined part of the following sentence?**

They always take such good care of <u>them</u> garden.

- Ⓐ  that
- Ⓑ  there
- Ⓒ  they're
- Ⓓ  their

**6. What is the correct way to write the underlined part of the sentence?**

Tony and Melissa had fun <u>sing</u> in the spring concert.

- Ⓐ sung
- Ⓑ singing
- Ⓒ sang
- Ⓓ will sing

**7. What is the correct way to write the underlined part of the sentence?**

Debbie always <u>did</u> her homework first thing when she gets home.

- Ⓐ does
- Ⓑ will do
- Ⓒ doesn't do
- Ⓓ didn't

**8. What is the correct way to write the underlined part of the sentence? Write your answer in the box given below.**

Mickey's brother always takes <u>him</u> toys.

**9. What is the correct way to write the underlined part of the sentence? Write your answer in the box given below.**

<u>Them</u> holiday lights are so pretty and sparkly.

**10. What is the correct way to write the underlined part of the sentence? Write your answer in the box given below.**

My dog always runs <u>happy</u> by my side.

# Chapter 4

## Lesson 7: Demonstrate Command of Capitalization

You can scan the QR code given below or use the url to access additional EdSearch resources including videos and mobile apps related to *Demonstrate Command of Capitalization*.

 *Demonstrate Command of Capitalization*

| URL | QR Code |
| --- | --- |
| http://www.lumoslearning.com/a/l62 |  |

**1. Choose the answer with the correct placement of capital letters for the sentence below.**

my doctor moved to phoenix, arizona.

- Ⓐ my doctor moved to phoenix, arizona.
- Ⓑ My doctor moved to Phoenix, Arizona.
- Ⓒ My doctor moved to phoenix, arizona.
- Ⓓ My doctor moved to phoenix, arizona.

**2. Choose the answer with the correct placement of capital letters for the sentence below.**

my mother called doctor billings to make an appointment for saturday.

- Ⓐ My mother called Doctor Billings to make an appointment for Saturday.
- Ⓑ my mother called doctor billings to make an appointment for Saturday.
- Ⓒ My mother called doctor billings to make an appointment for saturday.
- Ⓓ My mother called doctor Billings to make an appointment for Saturday.

**3. Choose the answer with the correct placement of capital letters for the sentence below.**

mother says he is the best doctor in santa maria.

- Ⓐ Mother says he is the best doctor in santa maria.
- Ⓑ Mother says he is the best doctor in Santa maria.
- Ⓒ Mother says he is the best doctor in Santa Maria.
- Ⓓ mother says he is the best Doctor in Santa maria.

**4. Choose the answer with the correct placement of capital letters for the sentence below.**

the principal made pablo captain of the safety patrol.

- Ⓐ The principal made pablo captain of the safety patrol.
- Ⓑ The principal made Pablo Captain of the Safety Patrol.
- Ⓒ The principal made pablo captain of the Safety Patrol.
- Ⓓ The principal made Pablo captain of the safety patrol.

**5. Choose the answer with the correct placement of capital letters for the sentence below.**

captain jones of the american legion spoke at martin luther king, jr. elementary school.

- Ⓐ Captain Jones of the American Legion spoke at Martin Luther King, Jr. Elementary School.
- Ⓑ Captain jones of the american legion spoke at martin luther king, jr. elementary school.
- Ⓒ Captain jones of the American Legion spoke at martin luther king, jr. elementary school.
- Ⓓ Captain jones of the American legion spoke at Martin luther king, Jr. elementary school.

**6. Choose the answer with the correct placement of capital letters for the sentence below.**

dad, can you help me for a minute?

   Ⓐ  dad, can you help me for a minute?
   Ⓑ  Dad, Can You help Me for a Minute?
   Ⓒ  Dad, can you help me for a Minute?
   Ⓓ  Dad, can you help me for a minute?

**7. Choose the answer with the correct placement of capital letters for the sentence below.**

mom said angela can spend the night on friday.

   Ⓐ  Mom said angela can spend the night on friday.
   Ⓑ  Mom said Angela can spend the night on Friday.
   Ⓒ  Mom said Angela can spend the night on friday.
   Ⓓ  Mom said Angela can spend the Night on friday.

**8. Choose the answer with the correct placement of capital letters for the sentence below.**

my grandma made a german chocolate cake for sunday dinner.

   Ⓐ  My grandma made a german chocolate cake for sunday dinner.
   Ⓑ  My Grandma made a german chocolate cake for sunday dinner.
   Ⓒ  My grandma made a German chocolate cake for Sunday dinner.
   Ⓓ  my grandma made a german chocolate cake for Sunday dinner.

**9. Choose the answer with the correct placement of capital letters for the sentence below.**

kathy barrett lives on stanley street next door to domino's pizza.

   Ⓐ  Kathy Barrett lives on Stanley Street next door to Domino's Pizza.
   Ⓑ  Kathy barrett lives on stanley street next door to domino's pizza.
   Ⓒ  Kathy Barrett lives on stanley street next door to domino's pizza.
   Ⓓ  Kathy barrett lives on stanley street next door to Domino's pizza.

**10. Choose the answer with the correct placement of capital letters for the sentence below.**

michael read the call of the wild in july.

   Ⓐ  michael read the call of the wild in July.
   Ⓑ  Michael read The Call of the Wild in July.
   Ⓒ  Michael read the call of the wild in july.
   Ⓓ  Michael read The call of the wild in july.

**11. Read the below sentence and rewrite it with correct placement of capital letters.**

Mike was born in New jersey on september 13th.

```
╭─────────────────────────────────────────╮
│                                         │
│                                         │
│                                         │
╰─────────────────────────────────────────╯
```

**12. Read the below sentence and rewrite it with correct placement of capital letters.**

i live in malibu, california.

```
╭─────────────────────────────────────────╮
│                                         │
│                                         │
│                                         │
╰─────────────────────────────────────────╯
```

**13. Read the below sentence and rewrite it with correct placement of capital letters.**

In italy, the italian bread tastes very good.

```
╭─────────────────────────────────────────╮
│                                         │
│                                         │
│                                         │
╰─────────────────────────────────────────╯
```

## Chapter 4

## Lesson 8: Demonstrate Command of Punctuation

You can scan the QR code given below or use the url to access additional EdSearch resources including videos and mobile apps related to *Demonstrate Command of Punctuation*.

 **Demonstrate Command of Punctuation**

| URL | QR Code |
|-----|---------|
| http://www.lumoslearning.com/a/l62 |  |

**1. Choose the answer with the correct punctuation for the sentence below.**

Hi, Mom I'm home called Robby as he walked through the door

- Ⓐ "Hi, Mom! I'm home," called Robby as he walked through the door.
- Ⓑ Hi, Mom I'm home called Robby as he walked through the door.
- Ⓒ Hi Mom I'm home, called Robby as he walked through the door.
- Ⓓ Hi Mom, I'm home, called Robby, as he walked through the door.

**2. Choose the answer with the correct punctuation for the sentence below.**

I had bananas oranges and cherries in the refrigerator but they're all gone

- Ⓐ I had bananas oranges and cherries in the refrigerator but they're all gone.
- Ⓑ I had bananas oranges and cherries in the refrigerator, but they're all gone.
- Ⓒ I had bananas, oranges, and cherries in the refrigerator, but they're all gone.
- Ⓓ I had bananas oranges and cherries, in the refrigerator, but they're all gone.

**3. Choose the answer with the correct punctuation for the sentence below.**

September is the busiest month of the year that's why it's my favorite

- Ⓐ September is the busiest month of the year; that's why it's my favorite.
- Ⓑ September is the busiest month of the year that's why it's my favorite.
- Ⓒ September, is the busiest month of the year, that's why it's my favorite.
- Ⓓ September is the busiest month of the year that's why it's my favorite!

**4. Choose the answer with the correct punctuation for the sentence below.**

Which one is Olivias jacket the teacher asked

- Ⓐ Which one is Olivias jacket the teacher asked?
- Ⓑ Which one is Olivia's jacket the teacher asked.
- Ⓒ "Which one is Olivia's jacket?" the teacher asked.
- Ⓓ Which one is Olivia's jacket the teacher asked!

**5. Choose the answer with the correct punctuation for the sentence below.**

New Years Day will be on January 1 2012

- Ⓐ New Years Day will be on January 1 2012.
- Ⓑ New Year's Day will be on January 1, 2012.
- Ⓒ New Years Day will be on January, 1, 2012.
- Ⓓ New Year's Day, will be on January 1, 2012.

**6. Choose the answer with the correct punctuation for the sentence below.**

I got into a great college which made my mom happy.

 Ⓐ  I got in, to a great college which made, my mom happy.
 Ⓑ  I got in to a great, college which made my mom, happy.
 Ⓒ  I got into a great college, which made my mom happy.
 Ⓓ  I got into a great college which, made my mom happy.

**7. Choose the answer with the correct punctuation for the sentence below.**

Joyce remembered to bring her bathing suit on vacation but she left her sun screen in Dallas Texas.

 Ⓐ  Joyce remembered to bring her bathing suit on vacation, but she left her sun screen in Dallas, Texas.
 Ⓑ  Joyce remembered to bring her bathing suit on vacation but she left her sun screen in Dallas, Texas.
 Ⓒ  Joyce remembered to bring her bathing suit on vacation, but she left her sun screen in Dallas Texas.
 Ⓓ  Joyce remembered to bring her bathing suit, on vacation, but she left her sun screen, in Dallas, Texas.

**8. Choose the answer with the correct punctuation for the sentence below.**

Have you ever been to Albany New York, or Flourtown Pennsylvania.

 Ⓐ  Have you ever been to Albany, New York, or Flourtown Pennsylvania?
 Ⓑ  Have you ever been to Albany, New York or Flourtown, Pennsylvania.
 Ⓒ  Have you ever been to Albany New York, or Flourtown, Pennsylvania.
 Ⓓ  Have you ever been to Albany, New York or Flourtown, Pennsylvania?

**9. Choose the answer with the correct punctuation for the sentence below.**

Ryan stated "you shouldnt bully other kids.

 Ⓐ  Ryan stated, you shouldn't bully other kids.
 Ⓑ  Ryan stated, "you shouldnt bully other kids"
 Ⓒ  Ryan stated, "you shouldnt bully other kids.
 Ⓓ  Ryan stated, "You shouldn't bully other kids."

**10. Rewrite the sentence below with correct punctuation.**

Michelle made pizza grilled cheese and tacos for lunch but she didnt realize it was only 10:00 a.m.

**11. Rewrite the sentence below with correct punctuation.**

The teacher said "lets read the poem now.

**12. Rewrite the sentence below with correct punctuation.**

My brother whispered its a surprise.

# Chapter 4

## Lesson 9: Correct Spelling

You can scan the QR code given below or use the url to access additional EdSearch resources including videos and mobile apps related to *Correct Spelling*.

 Search

### Correct Spelling

| URL | QR Code |
|-----|---------|
| http://www.lumoslearning.com/a/l62 |  |

**1. Choose the correct word that fits the blank:**

Grind the wheat to a powdery _____.

Ⓐ flower
Ⓑ flour
Ⓒ floor
Ⓓ floure

**2. Choose the correct word that fits the blank:**

Among all _____, my favorite is the pink rose.

Ⓐ floors
Ⓑ flour
Ⓒ flowers
Ⓓ floures

**3. Choose the correct word that fits the blank:**

The last _____ creaked as I stepped on to it.

Ⓐ stare
Ⓑ stair
Ⓒ steer
Ⓓ stiar

**4. Choose the correct word that fits in the blank:**

He _____ the ball and it flew forward.

Ⓐ through
Ⓑ threw
Ⓒ throw
Ⓓ any of the above

**5. Choose the answer with the correct set of words, in the given order, to fill in the blank in the sentence below.**

I am _____ fed up by all the noise in the city, and hence am heading to the countryside for some peace and _____.

Ⓐ quiet, quite
Ⓑ quite, quiet
Ⓒ quite, quite
Ⓓ quiet, quiet

spelled

**6. Choose the correctly spelt word to fill in the blank in the sentence below.**

Britney _____ a car for her 18th birthday.

- Ⓐ received
- Ⓑ recieved
- Ⓒ purschesed
- Ⓓ baught

**7. Choose the correctly spelt word to fill in the blank in the sentence below.**

The boy was very _____ about King Tut and Egypt.

- Ⓐ nowledgeable
- Ⓑ knowlegeable
- Ⓒ knowledgeable
- Ⓓ knoledgable

**8. Choose the correctly spelt word to fill in the blank in the sentence below.**

The black and white cat had really long _____.

- Ⓐ whiskers
- Ⓑ whisckers
- Ⓒ wisikers
- Ⓓ None of the above

**9. Choose the correctly spelt word to fill in the blank in the sentence below.**

My favorite_____ is a small Italian place on Elm Street.

- Ⓐ restrant
- Ⓑ resturannt
- Ⓒ restaurant
- Ⓓ restraent

**10. Choose the correctly spelt word to fill in the blank in the sentence below.**

The _____ of the school gave a student detention.

- Ⓐ principle
- Ⓑ princapal
- Ⓒ principel
- Ⓓ principal

**11. What do you call an instrument with which you can see far away objects in the sky?**

_____

**12. What do you call a proposed route of travel and a guidebook for a journey?**

_____

## Chapter 4

## Lesson 10: Vary Sentences

You can scan the QR code given below or use the url to access additional EdSearch resources including videos and mobile apps related to *Vary Sentences*.

 **Vary Sentences**

| URL | QR Code |
| --- | --- |
| http://www.lumoslearning.com/a/l63 |  |

**1. What is the best way to combine the following sentences?**

The oven temperature was too hot.  The cookies got burnt.

- Ⓐ   The oven temperature was too hot, the cookies got burnt.
- Ⓑ   The oven temperature was too hot because the cookies got burnt.
- Ⓒ   The oven temperature was too hot the cookies got burnt.
- Ⓓ   The oven temperature was too hot, so the cookies got burnt.

**2. What is the best way to combine the following sentences?**

Mike and Johnny wanted to play outside.  It was raining so they couldn't.

- Ⓐ   Mike and Johnny wanted to play outside, but it was raining.
- Ⓑ   Because of the rain, Mike and Johnny couldn't play outside.
- Ⓒ   Mike and Johnny wanted to play outside and it was raining so they couldn't.
- Ⓓ   Mike and Johnny wanted to play outside in the rain.

**3. What is the best way to combine the following sentences?**

I would like to have pizza at my party.  I would also like to have ice cream and chocolate cake.

- Ⓐ   I would like to have pizza at my party, and I would also like to have ice cream and chocolat cake.
- Ⓑ   I would like to have pizza at my party, and ice cream and chocolate cake.
- Ⓒ   I would like to have pizza, ice cream, and chocolate cake at my party.
- Ⓓ   At my party, I would like to have pizza and ice cream and chocolate cake.

**4. What is the best way to combine the following sentences?**

We should go to the mall.  After school.

- Ⓐ   After school, we should go to the mall.
- Ⓑ   We should go to the mall, after school.
- Ⓒ   We should go to the mall, and after school.
- Ⓓ   After school, to the mall we should go.

**5. Which is the best way to combine the following sentences?**

The cat chases the dog.  The dog chases the cat.

   Ⓐ  The cat chases the dog, and the dog chases the cat.
   Ⓑ  The cat chases the dog, but the dog chases the cat.
   Ⓒ  The cat chases the dog, the dog chases the cat.
   Ⓓ  The cat and dog chase each other.

**6. Which is the best way to combine the following sentences?**

Summer is nice.  Spring is my favorite.

   Ⓐ  Summer is nice, and spring is my favorite.
   Ⓑ  Summer is nice, spring is my favorite.
   Ⓒ  Summer is nice, but spring is my favorite.
   Ⓓ  Summer and spring are nice.

**7. Which is the best way to combine the following sentences?**

We will be going camping.  After school on Friday.

   Ⓐ  We will be going camping, and after school on Friday.
   Ⓑ  After school on Friday, we will be going camping.
   Ⓒ  After school on Friday we will be going camping.
   Ⓓ  Camping we are going after school on Friday.

**8. Which is the best way to combine the following sentences? Circle the correct answer choice**

Before the party I have to wash the dishes.  I also have to do the laundry.  And walk the dog.

   Ⓐ  Before the party I have to wash the dishes.  I also have to do the laundry and walk the dog.
   Ⓑ  Before the party I have to wash the dishes do the laundry and walk the dog.
   Ⓒ  Before the party, I have to wash the dishes, do the laundry and walk the dog.
   Ⓓ  I have to wash the dishes.  I also have to do the laundry and walk the dog. Before the party.

**9. Which is the best way to combine the following sentences? Circle the correct answer choice**

Lisa got a book.  She got it at the library.

   Ⓐ  Lisa got a book at the library.
   Ⓑ  Lisa got a book, and she got it at the library.
   Ⓒ  Lisa got a book, so she got it at the library.
   Ⓓ  At the library, Lisa got her book.

**10. Which is the best way to combine the following sentences? Circle the correct answer choice**

The puppy was soft and cuddly.  It was brown.

Ⓐ  The puppy was soft and cuddly, and it was brown.
Ⓑ  The brown puppy was soft and cuddly.
Ⓒ  The puppy was soft and cuddly and brown.
Ⓓ  The puppy was brown and it was soft and it was cuddly.

## Chapter 4

## Lesson 11: Maintain Consistency in Style and Tone

You can scan the QR code given below or use the url to access additional EdSearch resources including videos and mobile apps related to *Maintain Consistency in Style and Tone*.

 **ed)Search**   *Maintain Consistency in Style and Tone*

| URL | QR Code |
|---|---|
| http://www.lumoslearning.com/a/l63b |  |

**1. Which of the following sentences paints the clearest picture?**

Ⓐ Even though the sun was shining, Mary couldn't help but feel chilled by the cool morning breeze.
Ⓑ Even though the sun was shining, Mary was still cold.
Ⓒ The sun was shining but the breeze made Mary cold.
Ⓓ Mary was chilled on the sunny, yet breeze morning.

**2. Which of the following sentences uses the most descriptive words and style?**

Ⓐ As the darkness fell, Scott was scared of what might be out there.
Ⓑ As the darkness fell, Scott couldn't help but be wary of what might lurk out there in the shadows.
Ⓒ As the darkness fell, Scott was frightened by what he could not see.
Ⓓ Scott is scared of the dark.

**3. Which of the following sentences provides the most detail about the topic?**

Ⓐ Callie loved the smell of cookies.
Ⓑ Callie loved the smell of her mother's cookies.
Ⓒ Callie loved the smell of her mother's fresh baked cookies.
Ⓓ Callie loved the smell of her mother's fresh baked chocolate chip cookies.

**4. Which of the following sentences provides sufficient information in an efficient format?**

Ⓐ George Washington was the first president. He was also a general in the American Revolution
Ⓑ George Washington was not only the first president, but he was also a general in the American Revolution.
Ⓒ George Washington was a general and president.
Ⓓ George Washington was the first president and a general in the American Revolution.

**5. Which of the following sentences is most concise?**

Ⓐ I loved the movie. I just didn't like the surprise ending.
Ⓑ I loved the movie, and I just didn't like the surprise ending.
Ⓒ I loved the movie, but I just didn't like the surprise ending.
Ⓓ I loved the movie, but I didn't like the surprise ending.

**6. Which of the following sentences is the most concise and accurate?**

Ⓐ I'm so nervous for the play. What if I forget my lines? What if I fall down and everyone laughs at me?

Ⓑ I'm so nervous for the play. What if I forget my lines, fall down, and everyone laughs at me?

Ⓒ I'm so nervous for the play. What if I forget my lines or fall down and everyone laughs at me?

Ⓓ I am nervous that I will forget my lines. I am nervous I will fall down and everyone will laugh at me.

**7. Which of the following sentences provides the most imaginative style?**

Ⓐ After the dog got out of the yard, Freddie ran after it.

Ⓑ The dog got out of the yard. Freddie ran after it.

Ⓒ Freddie ran after the dog, after it got out of the yard.

Ⓓ The dog got out of the yard and Freddie ran after it.

**8. Which of the following sentences provides the most detailed concise expression of the events? Circle the correct answer choice.**

Ⓐ Seth and Iris walked on the beach. They collected sea shells.

Ⓑ As they walked along the beach, Seth and Iris collected sea shells.

Ⓒ Seth and Iris walked and collected sea shells.

Ⓓ At the beach, Seth and Iris walked. They also collected sea shells.

**9. Which of the following sentences is the most concise? Circle the correct answer choice.**

Ⓐ Beth thought the test was hard and difficult. Mary thought the test was easy.

Ⓑ While Beth thought the test was challenging, Mary thought it was easy.

Ⓒ Beth thought the test was hard and Mary thought it was easy.

Ⓓ Beth thought the test was hard and difficult, but Mary thought the test was easy.

**10. Which of the following sentences uses the smoothest and most concise language to describe the event? Circle the correct answer choice.**

Ⓐ The lights slowly darkened to signal the start of the movie. Mark and Anthony got excited.

Ⓑ The lights slowly darkened to signal the start of the movie, and Mark and Anthony got excited.

Ⓒ Mark and Anthony got excited when the lights slowly darkened to signal the start of the movie.

Ⓓ The lights went out so the movie could start. Mark and Anthony got excited.

## Chapter 4

## Lesson 12: Use Clues To Determine Multiple-meaning Words

You can scan the QR code given below or use the url to access additional EdSearch resources including videos and mobile apps related to *Use Clues To Determine Multiple-meaning Words*.

 **Use Clues To Determine Multiple-meaning Words**

| URL | QR Code |
|-----|---------|
| http://www.lumoslearning.com/a/l64 |  |

Crab and shrimp: they're not just for dinner anymore. A natural polymer found in the exoskeletons of crustaceans can keep your car cleaner. Never heard of chitosan? You may not be able to say that for long. Researchers in the School of Fashion and Textiles at RMIT are using the biopolymer, found in the exoskeletons of crustaceans such as crabs and shrimp, to coat the 100% polyester fabric used in automobiles. Combining fragrant oils with the polymer, which has the ability to form an antimicrobial film, creates a durable, fragrant finish in the fabric.

**1. Based on this passage, crabs and shrimp are _____.**

Ⓐ  dinner
Ⓑ  fragrant
Ⓒ  crustaceans
Ⓓ  polyester

A natural polymer found in the exoskeletons of crustaceans can keep your car cleaner. Researchers in the School of Fashion and Textiles at RMIT are using the biopolymer, found in the exoskeletons of crustaceans such as crabs and shrimp, to coat the 100% polyester fabric used in automobiles. Combining fragrance oils with the polymer, which has the ability to form an antimicrobial film, creates a durable, fragrant finish in the fabric.

**2. Based on the prefix "exo-," and prior knowledge about crabs and shrimp, an exoskeleton is probably: _____.**

Ⓐ  a skeleton that is outside the body
Ⓑ  a skeleton that is inside the body
Ⓒ  a soft skeleton
Ⓓ  a durable skeleton

Crab and shrimp: they're not just for dinner anymore. A natural polymer found in the exoskeletons of crustaceans can keep your car cleaner. Never heard of chitosan? You may not be able to say that for long. Researchers in the School of Fashion and Textiles at RMIT are using the biopolymer, found in the exoskeletons of crustaceans such as crabs and shrimp, to coat the 100% polyester fabric used in automobiles. Combining fragrance oils with the polymer, which has the ability to form an antimicrobial film, creates a durable, fragrant finish in the fabric.

**3. Based on the prefix "bio-," a biopolymer is probably: _____.**

Ⓐ  a chemical substance found in the earth
Ⓑ  a chemical substance found in a living thing
Ⓒ  a chemical substance found in water
Ⓓ  a chemical substance found in the air

Researchers at RMIT's School of Fashion and Textiles are developing anti-stain, antimicrobial, and anti-odor textiles that keep car interiors clean and sweet-smelling. But that's not all they've got up their sleeves: projects range from wearable technology to protective fabrics – even sports apparel that can monitor your performance.

**4. 'But that's not all they've got up their sleeves', could mean: _____.**

- Ⓐ  They have some more projects coming up
- Ⓑ  they have no other projects coming up
- Ⓒ  they have rolled up their sleeves
- Ⓓ  they have projects on sleeves

Researchers at RMIT's School of Fashion and Textiles are developing anti-stain, antimicrobial, and anti-odor textiles that keep car interiors clean and sweet-smelling.

**5. Anti-odor and sweet-smelling textiles are _____.**

- Ⓐ  stainless
- Ⓑ  fragrant
- Ⓒ  durable
- Ⓓ  smelly

My friends and I were up early that spring morning. We were going hiking up in the cliffs. We were hiking for 4 days and 3 nights. I was very excited about this trip because we were going to stay in log cabins built on huge strong trees and cliffs. These trees and cliffs were very old and housed a lot of animals and birds.

We began the first day of our hiking at the main office, and our captain briefed us about the trails we were taking and the things we could see and hear.

The first trail was called the "aerie" trail. It was called so because the cliffs here were very high and housed a lot of eagles' nests (called aeries). We started our hike at 9:00 am and reached our first log cabin, destination at around 6:00 pm. The cabin was large and airy. It was very refreshing to see these cabins and the beds. Once up in my cabin I sat on my bed and looked out the window. It was a sight to behold! From my window, I could see lots of aeries at the cliff tops. I could also see little baby eagles inside these aeries. One of them was so close that I could see about 3 baby eagles inside the nest. I moved close to the window and fell asleep watching these tiny little birds.

**6. In the above passage, what is the synonym for the word "housed"?**

- Ⓐ  attracted
- Ⓑ  held
- Ⓒ  accepted
- Ⓓ  none of the above

When Westinghouse, the inventor of the air brake was working on his great invention, he made an application for a trial of his device on the New York Central Railroad.

**7. Choose the meaning of the word "brake" according to the above sentence.**

Ⓐ  a weapon
Ⓑ  an instrument
Ⓒ  a mechanical device which makes a vehicle stop when pressed
Ⓓ  the pedal

**8. Choose the answer that contains opposites.**

Ⓐ  return, march
Ⓑ  alive, dead
Ⓒ  opened, broke
Ⓓ  collect, take

**9. The volume of traffic was high on the interstate.**
**In the above sentence, the meaning of volume is _____.**

Ⓐ  a unit of written material assembled together
Ⓑ  loudness of sound
Ⓒ  a roll of parchment
Ⓓ  the amount of space occupied

**10. The money in my savings account is earning some interest.**
**In the above sentence, the meaning of interest is _____.**

Ⓐ  a state of curiosity
Ⓑ  attention to something
Ⓒ  an extra amount
Ⓓ  a charge for a loan

**11. Choose the answer that contains opposites.**

Ⓐ  Accept, take
Ⓑ  Ancient, modern
Ⓒ  argue, disagree
Ⓓ  Arrive,come

## 12. Choose the answer that contains opposites.

Ⓐ Blunt, sharp
Ⓑ Careful, caring
Ⓒ Cold, cool
Ⓓ Dirty, gross

## 13. Choose the answer that contains opposites.

Ⓐ Cheap, poor
Ⓑ Early, awake
Ⓒ Domestic, foreign
Ⓓ East, north

## Chapter 4

### Lesson 13: Use Context Clues to Determine Word Meaning

You can scan the QR code given below or use the url to access additional EdSearch resources including videos and mobile apps related to Use Context Clues to Determine Word Meaning.

 Search

**Use Context Clues to Determine Word Meaning**

| URL | QR Code |
|---|---|
| http://www.lumoslearning.com/a/l64 |  |

Julio was happy and astounded when he won MVP for the soccer season.  He had been sure that Reuben or Carlos were going to be chosen.

**1. The word "astounded" in this context means: _____.**

Ⓐ disappointed
Ⓑ very surprised
Ⓒ satisfied
Ⓓ pleased

A spider web may look flimsy, but spider silk is actually five times stronger than steel. It is tougher, stronger, and more flexible than anything humans have been able to produce.

**2. The word "flimsy" in this context means: _____.**

Ⓐ beautiful
Ⓑ silky
Ⓒ weak
Ⓓ inflexible

New Jersey is on the east coast of the Mid-Atlantic region of the United States of America. It bordered by the Atlantic Ocean to the east and by Delaware to the southwest, Pennsylvania to the west, and New York to the north and northeast. Parts of the state are suburbs of New York City, just across the Hudson River to the northeast, and Philadelphia, just across the Delaware River on the southwest.

**3. In the above context, "bordered" means _____.**

Ⓐ surrounded by
Ⓑ marked by
Ⓒ differentiated by
Ⓓ separated by

Africa is a very diverse continent, with each country, or even each part of a country, having its own unique culture. While it is common for people in the West to refer to Africa as if it was a single country, one should remember the sheer size of the continent. Africa is not one country but 55 different countries, meaning that it is impossible to make generalizations about Africa as a whole.

**4. In the above context, "sheer" means _____.**

Ⓐ vast
Ⓑ transparent
Ⓒ unmixed
Ⓓ small

My dog is devoted to my family. He would never leave us.

**5. In the above context, "devoted" means _____**

- Ⓐ loyal
- Ⓑ loving
- Ⓒ unloving
- Ⓓ hated

It is always beneficial to eat your vegetables. That's why your doctor tells you to eat plenty of fruits and vegetables.

**6. In the above context, "beneficial" means _____**

- Ⓐ horrible
- Ⓑ wrong
- Ⓒ good for you
- Ⓓ nice

The stench coming from the garbage can was unbearable.

**7. In the above context, "stench" means _____**

- Ⓐ sugary
- Ⓑ freshness
- Ⓒ sweetness
- Ⓓ stink

The celebrity walked the red carpet and was overwhelmed by the barrage of questions from reporters.

**8. In the above context, "barrage" means _____**

- Ⓐ abundance
- Ⓑ few
- Ⓒ twenty
- Ⓓ little

The sweltering summer heat made the beach unpleasant.

**9. In the above context, "sweltering" means _____**

   Ⓐ  cold
   Ⓑ  frigid
   Ⓒ  hot
   Ⓓ  humid

The big, nasty creature was brown and hairy; it looked hideous.

**10. In the above context, "hideous" means _____**

Jon was reluctant to see the horror movie because he did not like scary things.

**11. In the above context, 'reluctant' means _____**

The clothes were saturated because they were left outside in the rain.

**12. In the above context, 'saturated' means _____**

# Chapter 4

## Lesson 14: Use Common Roots and Affixes

You can scan the QR code given below or use the url to access additional EdSearch resources including videos and mobile apps related to Use Common Roots and Affixes.

 **ed Search**

### Use Common Roots and Affixes

| URL | QR Code |
|-----|---------|
| http://www.lumoslearning.com/a/l64 |  |

## 1. Which of the following is a true statement?

Ⓐ A suffix or ending is an affix, which is placed at the end of a word.
Ⓑ A prefix or beginning is an affix, which is placed at the beginning of a word.
Ⓒ A suffix is attached at the beginning of the word.
Ⓓ Both A and B

## 2. When the suffix "-able" is added to the word "cap", it means-

Ⓐ able to do something
Ⓑ to do anything
Ⓒ not able to do something
Ⓓ not able to do anything

## 3. Identify the suffix in the following words:

Salvage, Storage, Forage

Ⓐ A
Ⓑ ge
Ⓒ age
Ⓓ rage

## 4. Identify the prefix in the following words.

Anarchy, Anonymous, Anemia

Ⓐ Anna
Ⓑ An
Ⓒ Ana
Ⓓ Both A and B

## 5. What does the suffix "less" mean?

Ⓐ Too little
Ⓑ With
Ⓒ Without
Ⓓ None of the above

**6. What does the suffix "ology" mean?**

Ⓐ  Study
Ⓑ  Vocabulary
Ⓒ  Sadness
Ⓓ  Study of animals

**7. Identify the meaning of the root word in the following words:**

Commemorate, Commune, Community

```




```

**8. Which of the following statements is true?**

Ⓐ  The first rule of decoding words is to find out if the word has any suffixes or prefixes
Ⓑ  You should always divide between the consonants
Ⓒ  Both A and B
Ⓓ  None of the above

**9. Using the rule 'divide between the consonants', decode the word 'sentence'.**

Ⓐ  se-n-tence
Ⓑ  sen-tence
Ⓒ  sen-ten-ce
Ⓓ  none of the above

**10. What is the correct way to decode the word 'Monarch'**

Ⓐ  mona-rch
Ⓑ  mon-ar-ch
Ⓒ  mon-a-rch
Ⓓ  mon-arch

**11. Identify the prefix in the following words:**

Diameter, diagnol, diabolical

**12. Identify the meaning of the root word in the following words:**

Recede, secede, precede

## Chapter 4

## Lesson 15: Consult Reference Materials

You can scan the QR code given below or use the url to access additional EdSearch resources including videos and mobile apps related to Consult Reference Materials.

 **Consult Reference Materials**

| URL | QR Code |
|---|---|
| http://www.lumoslearning.com/a/l64 |  |

## 1. Alphabetize the following words:

hibiscus, petunia, rose, honeysuckle, daffodil

- (A) hibiscus, petunia, rose, honeysuckle, daffodil
- (B) daffodil, hibiscus, honeysuckle, petunia, rose
- (C) daffodil, honeysuckle, hibiscus, petunia, rose
- (D) hibiscus, petunia, rose, daffodil, honeysuckle

## 2. Alphabetize the following words:

mouse, mule, monkey, moose, mole

- (A) mouse, monkey, moose, mole, mule
- (B) mouse, mule, monkey, moose, mole
- (C) mouse, moose, monkey, mole, mule
- (D) mole, monkey, moose, mouse, mule

## 3. Alphabetize the following words:

sustain, solicit, sizzle, sanitize, secure

- (A) sustain, solicit, sizzle, sanitize, secure
- (B) sanitize, secure, sustain, solicit, sizzle
- (C) sanitize, solicit, sizzle, sustain, secure
- (D) sanitize, secure, sizzle, solicit, sustain

## 4. The dictionary contains _____.

- (A) meaning of a word
- (B) pronunciation of a word
- (C) the etymology (where the word came from)
- (D) all the above

## 5. Which of the following answer choices can you find in a thesaurus?

- (A) homonym
- (B) homograph
- (C) synonym
- (D) definition

**6. How do you go about starting to find a word you are looking for in the dictionary?**

Ⓐ  Open the dictionary
Ⓑ  Open the dictionary to the page that has the first two letters of the word you are looking for
Ⓒ  Open the dictionary to the page that has the last two letters of the word
Ⓓ  Open the dictionary and look in the table of contents

**7. What are guidewords in a dictionary?**

Ⓐ  Guidewords are words that tell you how to pronounce your word
Ⓑ  Guidewords are located at the bottom of each page
Ⓒ  Guidewords are words that tell you the part of speech of your word
Ⓓ  Guidewords are at the top of each page to tell you the first and last words you will find on that page.

**8. How many syllables are in the word "organized?"**

**9. How many syllables are in the word "jacket?"**

Ⓐ  1
Ⓑ  3
Ⓒ  2
Ⓓ  4

**10. How many syllables would you have, if you divide the word 'hyacinth'?**

Ⓐ  2
Ⓑ  3
Ⓒ  8
Ⓓ  4

**11. Alphabetize the following words as they are found in a dictionary and write it in the correct sequence in the boxes given below:**

obscure, obsess, obligation, objective

| | | | |
|---|---|---|---|
| | | | |

**12. Alphabetize the following words as they are found in a dictionary and write it in the correct sequence in the boxes given below:**

hesitate, hence, hibernate, hero

| | | | |
|---|---|---|---|
| | | | |

## Chapter 4

### Lesson 16: Determine the Meaning of a Word

You can scan the QR code given below or use the url to access additional EdSearch resources including videos and mobile apps related to *Determine the Meaning of a Word*.

## *Determine the Meaning of a Word*

| URL | QR Code |
|-----|---------|
| http://www.lumoslearning.com/a/l64 |  |

## 1. What does the underlined word in the sentence mean?

Johnny was certain he hadn't <u>misplaced</u> his glove but he couldn't find it.

- Ⓐ found
- Ⓑ lost
- Ⓒ hid
- Ⓓ borrowed

## 2. What does the underlined word in the sentence mean?

Despite the <u>brisk</u> temperatures, football fans still packed the stadium to watch the championship game.

- Ⓐ hot
- Ⓑ fast
- Ⓒ cool
- Ⓓ exciting

## 3. What does the underlined word in the sentence mean?

Natalie and Sophia couldn't wait to ride the roller coaster.  They'd heard it was very <u>exhilarating</u>.

- Ⓐ fast
- Ⓑ frightening
- Ⓒ exciting
- Ⓓ boring

## 4. What does the underlined word in the sentence mean? Circle the correct answer choice

Billy always found raking leaves to be a very <u>mundane</u> chore. It was the same thing over and over.

- Ⓐ fun
- Ⓑ challenging
- Ⓒ easy
- Ⓓ boring

## 5. What does the underlined word in the sentence mean? Circle the correct answer choice

The whimpering puppies were clearly <u>ravenous</u>. They devoured the food when it was ready.

- Ⓐ hungry
- Ⓑ sleepy
- Ⓒ playful
- Ⓓ scared

## 6. What does the underlined word in the sentence mean?

The basketball team had <u>triumphed</u> over their opponents.

- Ⓐ lost
- Ⓑ forfeited
- Ⓒ competed
- Ⓓ won

## 7. What does the underlined word in the sentence mean?

Abby found the new student to be <u>bewitching</u>.

- Ⓐ scary
- Ⓑ charming
- Ⓒ kind
- Ⓓ boring

## 8. What does the underlined word in the sentence mean?

Julia found fishing to be completely <u>repulsing</u>. She wanted nothing to do with putting the worm on the hook.

- Ⓐ wonderful
- Ⓑ delightful
- Ⓒ relaxing
- Ⓓ awful

## 9. What does the underlined word in the sentence mean?

As Tony and Steve climbed higher and higher up the mountainside, they noticed everything took on a whole new <u>perspective</u>.

- Ⓐ appearance
- Ⓑ experience
- Ⓒ height
- Ⓓ altitude

## 10. If you do not know what a word means, where can you look?

- Ⓐ Dictionary
- Ⓑ Thesaurus
- Ⓒ Glossary
- Ⓓ All of the above

## Chapter 4

## Lesson 17: Interpret Figures of Speech

You can scan the QR code given below or use the url to access additional EdSearch resources including videos and mobile apps related to Interpret Figures of Speech.

### Interpret Figures of Speech

| URL | QR Code |
|-----|---------|
| http://www.lumoslearning.com/a/l65 |  |

**1. What type(s) of figurative language is(are) being used in the sentence below?**

Jimmy and Johnny jumped like jelly beans.

- Ⓐ Metaphor
- Ⓑ Idiom
- Ⓒ Personification
- Ⓓ Alliteration

**2. What type of figurative language is being used in the sentence below?**

Don't spill the beans.

- Ⓐ Idiom
- Ⓑ Onomatopoeia
- Ⓒ Personification
- Ⓓ Alliteration

**3. What type of figurative language is being used in the sentence below?**

That sandwich is as big as a car.

- Ⓐ Personification
- Ⓑ Simile
- Ⓒ Metaphor
- Ⓓ Alliteration

**4. What type of figurative language is being used in the sentence below?**

We better cook a lot of food; we have an army to feed.

- Ⓐ Hyperbole
- Ⓑ Alliteration
- Ⓒ Idiom
- Ⓓ Personification

**5. What type of figurative language is being used in the sentence below?**

The baby bear looked up at its mother with adoring eyes filled with love.

- Ⓐ Idiom
- Ⓑ Alliteration
- Ⓒ Personification
- Ⓓ Metaphor

**6. What type of figurative language is being used in the sentence below?**

Zoom, roared the car engine.

Ⓐ  Personification
Ⓑ  Simile
Ⓒ  Idiom
Ⓓ  Onomatopoeia

**7. What type of figurative language is being used in the sentence below?**

Katy is a pig when she eats.

Ⓐ  Simile
Ⓑ  Metaphor
Ⓒ  Onomatopoeia
Ⓓ  Alliteration

**8. What type of figurative language is being used in the sentence below?**

Yesterday was the worst day of my entire life.

Ⓐ  Alliteration
Ⓑ  Hyperbole
Ⓒ  Idiom
Ⓓ  Simile

**9. What type of figurative language is being used in the sentence below? Enter your answer in the box given below**

Stop pulling my leg..

**10. What type of figurative language is being used in the sentence below? Enter your answer in the box given below**

Danielle's dancing is as graceful as a swan.

**11. Match the figure of speech with it's example**

( The fire swallowed the entire forest )   ( He is as cunning as a fox )   ( The world is a stage )

| simile |
| Metaphor |
| Personification |

## Chapter 4

## Lesson 18: Use Relationships to Better Understand Words

You can scan the QR code given below or use the url to access additional EdSearch resources including videos and mobile apps related to Use Relationships to Better Understand Words.

 **Use Relationships to Better Understand Words**

| URL | QR Code |
|-----|---------|
| http://www.lumoslearning.com/a/l65 |  |

**. Identify the cause and the effect in the following sentence:**

The blizzard was so widespread that all flights were cancelled.

cause _____ effect _____

  Ⓐ   cause-blizzard; effect- flights cancelled
  Ⓑ   cause-flights; effect- blizzard
  Ⓒ   cause-blizzard; effect- flights
  Ⓓ   cause-cancelled flights; effect- widespread blizzard

**. Identify the cause and the effect in the following sentence:**

Several hundred people were left homeless by the flood.

cause _____ effect _____

  Ⓐ   cause- homeless people; effect -flood
  Ⓑ   cause- flood; effect - people left homeless
  Ⓒ   cause- people; effect -homeless
  Ⓓ   cause- flood; effect -several hundred people

**. Identify the cause and the effect in the following sentence:**

Pedro's friendly attitude got him the job.

cause _____ effect _____

  Ⓐ   cause- Pedro; effect- friendly attitude
  Ⓑ   cause- Pedro; effect- got the job
  Ⓒ   cause- friendly attitude; effect- got the job
  Ⓓ   cause- job; effect- friendly attitude

**. Choose the correct animal which belongs to the category of mammals:** _____

  Ⓐ   giraffe
  Ⓑ   cheese
  Ⓒ   frogs
  Ⓓ   bees

5. **Choose the correct item which belongs to the category of birds:** _____

   Ⓐ  parrots
   Ⓑ  giraffes
   Ⓒ  bees
   Ⓓ  sharks

6. **Choose the correct item which belongs to the category of desserts:** _____

   Ⓐ  elephants
   Ⓑ  pie
   Ⓒ  carrots
   Ⓓ  cheese

7. **This exercise will help you practice identifying parts and wholes.**
   **Arrange the following words in order by size:**

galaxy, universe, county, country, town, neighborhood, state, world, continent, solar system hemisphere.

A street is part of a _____,
which is part of a _____,
which is part of a _____,
which is part of a _____,
which is part of a _____,
which is part of a _____,
which is part of a _____,
which is part of a _____,
which is part of a _____,
which is part of a _____,
which is part of a _____,
which is part of a _____.

   Ⓐ  town; neighborhood; county; state; country; continent; galaxy; hemisphere; world; universe solar system
   Ⓑ  world; solar system; galaxy; universe; neighborhood; town; county; state; country; continent hemisphere;
   Ⓒ  neighborhood; town; county; state; country; continent; hemisphere; world; solar system galaxy; universe
   Ⓓ  neighborhood; galaxy; universe; town; county; state; country; hemisphere; world; solar system continent

**8. Choose the correct item which belongs to the category of insects: _____**

- Ⓐ sharks
- Ⓑ bees
- Ⓒ frogs
- Ⓓ parrots

**9. Identify the cause and the effect in the following sentence:**

The burned popcorn made the whole house smell like smoke.

cause _____ effect _____

- Ⓐ cause-popcorn; effect- smoke
- Ⓑ cause- burned popcorn; effect- smoky smell
- Ⓒ cause-house; effect- burned popcorn
- Ⓓ cause-smoky smell; effect- burned popcorn

**10. Identify the cause and the effect in the following sentence:**

He practiced until he could make 3 out of 4 free throws.

cause _____ effect _____

- Ⓐ cause- free throws; effect-practice
- Ⓑ cause- practice; effect- four free throws
- Ⓒ cause- practice; effect- make three out of four free throws
- Ⓓ cause- free throws; effect- three throws

**11. Identify the cause and the effect in the following sentence:**

The evenings are longer during Daylight Saving Time.

cause _____ effect _____

**12. Identify the cause and the effect in the following sentence:**

Whistling while you work makes the task easier.

cause _____ effect _____

**13. Identify the cause and the effect in the following sentence:**

The street sweeper makes a lot of noise.

cause _____ effect _____

## Chapter 4

### Lesson 19: Distinguish Between Word Associations and Definitions

You can scan the QR code given below or use the url to access additional EdSearch resources including videos and mobile apps related to Distinguish Between Word Associations and Definitions.

 **Distinguish Between Word Associations and Definitions**

| URL | QR Code |
|-----|---------|
| http://www.lumoslearning.com/a/l65 |  |

**1. Denotation of a word is the _____.**

  (A) slang for a word.
  (B) literal meaning.
  (C) part of speech of a word.
  (D) feelings we have about a word.

**2. Connotation refers to _____.**

  (A) the literal meaning of a word.
  (B) the part of speech of a word.
  (C) how we feel about a word.
  (D) the slang meaning of a word.

**3. Which of the following words has the same denotative meaning as the word house?**

  (A) dwelling
  (B) abode
  (C) residence
  (D) All of the above

**4. Which of the following words has the same denotative meaning as the word child?**

  (A) elderly
  (B) ancient
  (C) adolescent
  (D) None of the above

**5. Which of the following words have the same denotation?**

  (A) smelly; smiley
  (B) sweet; sweat
  (C) trash; garbage
  (D) stubborn; easy-going

**6. Which of the following words have the same denotation?**

  (A) expensive; cheap
  (B) short; tall
  (C) rabbit; horse
  (D) curious; nosy

The word "inexpensive" has a positive connotation.

**7. Which of the following words has the same denotation but a negative connotation?**

Ⓐ costly
Ⓑ expensive
Ⓒ free
Ⓓ cheap

The word "disaster" has a negative connotation.

**8. Which of the following words has the same denotation but a positive connotation?**

Ⓐ Catastrophe
Ⓑ Flop
Ⓒ Emergency
Ⓓ Tragedy

9. The word "messy" has a positive connotation.

**Which of the following words has the same denotation but a negative connotation? Circl the correct answer choice**

Ⓐ Filthy
Ⓑ Disorganized
Ⓒ Muddled
Ⓓ Sloppy

The word "old" has a negative connotation.

**10. Which of the following words has the same denotation but a positive connotation? Circl the correct answer choice**

Ⓐ Decrepit
Ⓑ Ancient
Ⓒ Elderly
Ⓓ Over the hill

## Chapter 4

## Lesson 20: Use Grade Appropriate Words

You can scan the QR code given below or use the url to access additional EdSearch resources including videos and mobile apps related to Use Grade Appropriate Words.

 Search

### Use Grade Appropriate Words

| URL | QR Code |
| --- | --- |
| http://www.lumoslearning.com/a/l66 |  |

The word "racket" has multiple meanings.

**1. Which sentence uses the word "racket" where it means "noise?"**

   Ⓐ  I nearly forgot my racket before tennis practice.
   Ⓑ  There was a lot of racket coming from my brother's room.
   Ⓒ  My racket broke when I dropped it down the stairs.
   Ⓓ  I hope I get a new racket for my birthday.

The word "bear" has multiple meanings.

**2. Which sentence uses the word "bear" where it means "to hold up?"**

   Ⓐ  The baby bear is so cute!
   Ⓑ  I cannot bear to see someone hurt.
   Ⓒ  That apple tree sure does bear a lot of fruit.
   Ⓓ  I can't bear to stand on my broken ankle.

The word "patient" has multiple meanings.

**3. Which sentence uses the word "patient" where it means "quietly waiting?"**

   Ⓐ  The doctor sent the patient for x-rays of her wrist.
   Ⓑ  The nurse checked on the patient frequently.
   Ⓒ  The little boy is being very patient in line.
   Ⓓ  The patient needs to go home and rest before he feels better.

The word "pound" has multiple meanings.

**4. Which sentence uses the word "pound" where it means "to hit?"**

   Ⓐ  We got our new dog from the pound.
   Ⓑ  Jimmy had to pound on the box to get it to break open.
   Ⓒ  The watermelon weighs 16 pounds!
   Ⓓ  Sixteen ounces is equal to one pound.

The word "pack" has multiple meanings.

**5. Which sentence uses the word "pack" where it means "a group of animals?"**

Ⓐ  Did you see that pack of wolves down in the valley?
Ⓑ  Don't forget to pack your toothbrush.
Ⓒ  I packed a sandwich, an apple, and a cookie in your lunch.
Ⓓ  Marissa put her pack on her back.

**6. Which of the following words best complete the sentence?**

Even though I studied, I feel very _____ about the test in Science.

Ⓐ  excited
Ⓑ  anxious
Ⓒ  happy
Ⓓ  ready

**7. Which of the following words best completes the sentence?**

I can't believe how _____ the Grand Canyon is.

Ⓐ  immense
Ⓑ  small
Ⓒ  brown
Ⓓ  stationary

**8. Which of the following words best completes the sentence?**

They say the race is very _____ , so I had better spend some extra time training.

Ⓐ  easy
Ⓑ  smooth
Ⓒ  distinct
Ⓓ  rigorous

**9. Which of the following words best completes the sentence? Circle the correct answer choice**

Joey got himself into quite a _____ when he cheated on the test.

Ⓐ  predicament
Ⓑ  problem
Ⓒ  challenge
Ⓓ  bit of luck

**10. Which of the following words best completes the sentence? Circle the correct answe choice**

The team was very _____ about practicing.

- (A) lazy
- (B) sloppy
- (C) successful
- (D) diligent

# End of Language

# Answer Key and Detailed Explanations

## Chapter 4: Language

# Lesson 1: Correct Subject-Verb Agreement

| Question No. | Answer | Detailed Explanations |
|---|---|---|
| 1 | B | The subject is plural (Tracy and Gary), so there needs to be a plural verb (one with no "s" on the end.) |
| 2 | B | "All" is a plural subject, so you need a plural verb (one without an "s".) |
| 3 | B | The subject of the sentence is people, which is plural. That means the verb needs to be plural (which means that the verb does not have an "s".) |
| 4 | D | Answer choice D is correct. The other three do not sound right if you read them carefully. |
| 5 | B | B is the correct answer. If you read all of the answer choices carefully, B is the only one that sounds correct. |
| 6 | B | B is the correct answer. Some is the plural subject of the sentence, so you need a plural verb (one without an "s".) Seem is the only one that sounds correct. |
| 7 | A | "All" is the plural subject of the sentence, so you need a plural verb (one with no "s".) That is why A "appear" is the correct answer. |
| 8 | B | Answer choice B is correct. "Parents and students" is the plural subject, so you need a plural verb (which is "are"). |
| 9 | C | Either is a singular subject, so you need a singular verb (which is "has".) |
| 10 | C | The correct answer is C. "There are things" is the way it should read. If it was only one THING, then it would read "There is a thing." |
| 11 | The girl's shirt is lime green. | There is one girl. We know that because it is girl's and not girls'. That means the subject is singular, so the verb must be singular too (which means the verb does not have an "s".) |
| 12 | Tony climbs the tree every day after school. | Tony is one person (singular subject), so it needs a singular verb (one with an "s".) |
| 13 | The team is going to win the game. | The team is a collective noun and is functioning as one person. That makes the subject singular, which means it needs a singular verb |

# Lesson 2: Correct Use of Adjectives and Adverbs

| Question No. | Answer | Detailed Explanations |
|---|---|---|
| 1 | A | The answer is A, colorful. Adjectives are words that describe nouns, and colorful describes the pages. Reading is a verb (with the helping verb was.) Pages and book are both nouns because they are things. |
| 2 | B | The answer is B. Adjectives are words that describe nouns, and beautiful describes the noun planet. Earth is a proper noun and both system and planet are nouns. |
| 3 | C | The correct answer is C. Alien and airship are both nouns and ran is a verb. Frightened is the only describing word. |
| 4 | A | The answer is A. Adverbs answer the questions **how, how often, when, where, how much, or to what extent.** "Quite" shows to what extent the mother was unhappy. |
| 5 | D | The answer is D. Adverbs answer the questions **how, how often, when, where, how much, or to what extent**. Utterly shows to what extent the man was tired. |
| 6 | C | The answer is C. Once you find the verb (which is answered), ask yourself, "How were all of the questions answered?" "They were answered correctly." That's how you find the adverb. |
| 7 | politely | Adverbs answer the questions **how, how often, when, where, how much, or to what extent**. "politely" This tells us **how** the girl asked for her book. |
| 8 | D | The answer is D. "Polka dot" and "cold" are both adjectives (or describing words) that describe the nouns "umbrella" and "rain." Protected is a verb, so these are the only two choices for adjectives. |
| 9 | A | Adverbs answer the questions **how, how often, when, where, how much, or to what extent**. The answer is A, "soundly." This modifies the verb "slept" and tells us HOW the family slept. |
| 10 | hardly | Adverbs answer the questions **how, how often, when, where, how much, or to what extent**. "hardly" This tells us **to what extent** the printer works. |
| 11 | really | It modifies the word "busy" and tells us how busy Peter is. |

# Lesson 3: Recognize Pronouns

| Question No. | Answer | Detailed Explanations |
|---|---|---|
| 1 | B | Answer choice B is correct. "Myself" is a reflexive pronoun. None of the other answer choices sound correct. |
| 2 | B | The correct answer is B, "ourselves", because "we" is the subject. That tells us that it is more than one person and the author is included in the decorations. |
| 3 | B | Because "she" is used in the sentence, we know the answer is B "herself". The other three answers do not make sense in the sentence. |
| 4 | B | The correct answer is B. "A student" is the referent of the pronoun in the sentence. That's how we know to use "he or she has" in the blank. "You" does not make sense because its 2nd person, and "a student" is 3rd person. For that reason, it can't be A or C. "They" is 3rd person, but is referring to more than one person. |
| 5 | C | The correct answer is C. The referent of the pronoun is "players", so we know the pronoun should be plural. "Her", "its", and "his" are all singular pronouns. |
| 6 | A | They mention that Carol is his friend, so we know that Sue is his girlfriend. The answer is A. |
| 7 | B | It mentions that riding without a helmet is a risk. We know from that, what the risk is. The answer is B. |
| 8 | B | The tragedy mentioned (the cat eating the goldfish) is what was terrible, so the answer is B. |
| 9 | Johnny has grown a lot this year. | Since it says Johnny is taller than Ahmed, then we know they are talking about how much Johnny has grown. |
| 10 | A | The Sharks and Jets performed great dances, so they is appropriate. The answer is A. |
| 11 | Carrots give you vitamin A. | The sentence is saying that carrots are better, and one of the reasons is that they give you vitamin A. |
| 12 | Walking and running are fun, too. | You have to say "walking and running" again. Otherwise, it is not clear if they are talking about "walking and running" or "team sports". |

# Lesson 4: Recognize and Correct Shifts in Pronoun

| Question No. | Answer | Detailed Explanations |
|---|---|---|
| 1 | | Since each student is singular, his/her will be the correct answer. |
| 2 | | While we know that her is a pronoun for girl, it is still not the correct answer choice because the sentence references girls (plural) and her is a singular pronoun. Their is the correct word. |
| 3 | | Since we know that Coach Bob is a boy and is singular, the correct answer would be "his." |
| 4 | A | The only answer choice that is grammatically correct is A, I. "Billy and me," does not sound right, nor does "Billy and us" or "Billy and his." |
| 5 | C | Since the sentence is talking about Mrs. Marshall's students, which is a collective grouping of students, we need to look for an answer choice which is plural. The best answer choice is C, "they." |
| 6 | D | Since Johnny is a boy, we need to find an answer which reflects this. The best choice is answer D, "him." |
| 7 | A | Since Lucy is a girl, we know we are looking for a pronoun that represents a girl. The correct answer is A, "her." |
| 8 | C | When talking about Aunt Sara, the sentence says "my" which means one. Therefore, answer choices A and D will not work because they are both plurals. "He" isn't quite right because we don't know who he is. The correct answer choice is C, "I." |
| 9 | A | Since Tiffany is a girl, we are looking for an answer that supports this. "Her" doesn't sound right, so "she," answer A, is the correct answer. |
| 10 | C | The sentence talks about one dog who likes playing catch with his ball, therefore we are looking for a pronoun that is singular and male. The correct answer is C, "he." |

# Lesson 5: Recognize and Correct Vague Pronouns

| Question No. | Answer | Detailed Explanations |
|---|---|---|
| 1 | A | The antecedent in the sentence is anybody, which is singular, therefore the correct pronoun would be his. The correct answer is A. |
| 2 | B | The antecedent in the sentence is students, which is plural, therefore the correct pronoun would be their. No other pronoun makes sense. The correct answer is B |
| 3 | D | The antecedent in the sentence is Gavin, which is a single boy, therefore the correct pronoun would be him. The correct answer is D. |
| 4 | A | The antecedents in the sentence are Emily and Nathan. Since there are two of them, the correct pronoun needs to be plural. The correct answer is A, they. |
| 5 | A | The antecedent in the sentence is students, which is plural, therefore the correct pronoun would be their. There would not be correct because it is not the correct use of the word. No other pronouns make sense. The correct answer is A. |
| 6 | B | The antecedent in the sentence is Roger. Since Roger is a single boy, the correct pronoun would be B, his. |
| 7 | them | The antecedent in the sentence is cookies, which is plural. Hence, the only pronoun which makes sense is them. |
| 8 | its | The antecedent in the sentence is store, which is singular. The correct pronoun would be its. No other pronoun makes sense. |
| 9 | she | The antecedent in the sentence is Patty. Since Patty is a singular girl, the correct pronoun is she. |
| 10 | D | The antecedents in the story are Billy and Luis. Since there are two of them, the pronoun should represent two individuals not one. The only pronoun that correctly completes the sentence is D, their. |

# Lesson 6: Recognize Variations in English

| Question No. | Answer | Detailed Explanations |
|---|---|---|
| 1 | D | The sentence says that mom made cookies yesterday which means it happened in the past. Therefore, you need to find an answer that is written in the past tense.  Answer choice B is future. Answer choices A, C, and D are all past but only D makes sense. The correct answer is D. |
| 2 | A | The word "went" tells us this sentence is written in past tense. The only answer that is in past tense and makes sense is A, "bought." |
| 3 | B | While they're sounds right, the correct word would actually be their as it shows possession. They're represents 'they are' and that would not make sense in the sentence. The correct answer is B. |
| 4 | A | This sentence references something that will happen in the future.  Answer choice A, "will build" makes the most sense and references something that will happen in the future. |
| 5 | D | With this sentence, we are looking for a word that will go along with "they" because the garden belongs to someone which tells us that we want to find a possessive word. The best answer choice is D, "their." |
| 6 | B | The answer choice that sounds the best is B, singing. |
| 7 | A | We are looking for a positive word that makes sense in the sentence. The best choice is A, "does." |
| 8 | his | Since Mickey's brother takes Mickey's toys we are looking for a pronoun to replace Mickey. |
| 9 | those | The sentence is referencing a specific group of holiday lights. |
| 10 | happily | The correct adverb to complete the sentence is "happily." |

# Lesson 7: Demonstrate Command of Capitalization

| Question No. | Answer | Detailed Explanations |
|---|---|---|
| 1 | B | Answer choice B is correct. The beginning of the sentence should be capitalized. Also the city and state should be capitalized. |
| 2 | A | The correct answer is A. "My should be capitalized because it's the beginning of the sentence. "Doctor Billings" should be capitalized because that's his name. Saturday should be capitalized because it's one of the days of the week. |
| 3 | C | Answer choice C is correct. "Mother" should be capitalized because it is the beginning of the sentence. "Santa Maria" should be capitalized because it's a proper noun, the name of a place. "Doctor" should not be capitalized because it's not the name of a specific doctor. |
| 4 | D | "The" should be capitalized because it's the beginning of the sentence, but "principal" should not be capitalized. If it were "Principal Phillips" then it would be capitalized, because it would be a specific principal. "Pablo" should be capitalized because it's a person's name. The words "safety patrol" and "captain" should not be capitalized because they're not proper nouns. |
| 5 | A | Answer choice A is correct. "Captain Jones" is the name of a specific captain, so it should be capitalized. "American Legion" is a proper noun, and so is "Martin Luther King Jr. Elementary School." Therefore, they should both be capitalized. |
| 6 | D | Dad is the only proper noun in the sentence which needs to be capitalized. |
| 7 | B | Answer choice B is correct. The proper nouns are "Mom", "Angela", and "Friday". |
| 8 | C | Answer choice C is correct. "My" should be capitalized because it's the beginning of the sentence. German should be capitalized because it is a nationality, even though it is talking about a type of cake. Sunday should be capitalized because it is the day of the week. |
| 9 | A | Answer choice A is correct. "Kathy Barrett" should be capitalized because it's a name. "Stanley Street" is the name of the street, and "Dominos" is the name of the restaurant. |
| 10 | B | Answer choice B is correct. "Michael" should be capitalized because it's a name. "The Call and Wild" is capitalized because it's a title and "July" should be capitalized because it's one of the months of the year. |

| Question No. | Answer | Detailed Explanations |
|---|---|---|
| 11 | Mike was born in New Jersey on September 13th. | Mike, New Jersey and September are all proper nouns. |
| 12 | I live in Malibu, California. | Malibu and California should be capitalized because they are proper nouns. |
| 13 | In Italy, the Italian bread tastes very good. | Italy should be capitalized because it is a country, and Italian should be capitalized because it's the name of a nationality. |

# Lesson 8: Demonstrate Command of Punctuation

| Question No. | Answer | Detailed Explanations |
|:---:|:---:|:---|
| 1 | A | You must have quotations around what is said out loud. For that reason, answer choice A is correct. |
| 2 | C | Answer choice C is correct. There are two comma rules in place here. There needs to be a comma in items in a series (bananas, oranges, and cherries) and there is a compound sentence, so there needs to be a comma before the but. |
| 3 | A | Answer choice A is correct. There needs to be a semicolon after year because there are two complete sentences. You can't just put them together with a comma. It has to be a comma and a conjunction or a semicolon. |
| 4 | C | Answer choice C is correct. There has to be quotation marks around anything that is said out loud. |
| 5 | B | The only comma should be between the day and year. An apostrophe is used in Year's because year is a singular day. |
| 6 | C | The correct answer is C. The only comma that is needed is between the two clauses. "Which made my mom happy" is a dependent clause and the other clause is independent. It needs a conjunction or to be set apart in commas. |
| 7 | A | The correct answer is A. This is a compound sentence, so there needs to be a comma between vacation and but. Also, there needs to be a comma between the city and state (Dallas, Texas.) |
| 8 | D | There must always be a comma between the city and state. There should be a comma after Albany and a comma after Flourtown. Since the sentence is a question, it should end with a question mark rather than a period. |
| 9 | D | Answer choice D is correct because it's the only one where the You is capitalized. Any time a new sentence is used in dialogue, the first word in the sentence needs to be capitalized. There should also be an apostrophe in the contraction shouldn't. |
| 10 | | Michelle made pizza, grilled cheese, and tacos for lunch, but she didn't realize it was only 10:00 a.m.<br><br>There should be commas in the items in a series (pizza, grilled cheese, and tacos) and there should be a comma before but (because it's a compound sentence). There should also be an apostrophe in the word didn't because it is a contraction for the words did not. |

| Question No. | Answer | Detailed Explanations |
|---|---|---|
| 11 | | The teacher said, "lets read the poem now".There should be a comma to introduce the quote, quotations around the quote, and a period before the end of the quote. |
| 12 | | My brother whispered," its a surprise"."It's a surprise" is what my brother whispered out loud, so that's what needs to be in the quotation marks. |

# Lesson 9: Correct Spelling

| Question No. | Answer | Detailed Explanations |
|---|---|---|
| 1 | B | Answer choice B is correct because that is the correct spelling of the flour that you cook with. This type of flour is made from grinding wheat. |
| 2 | C | Answer choice C is the correct word for the type of flowers mentioned in the sentence. The other options do not make sense in the sentence. |
| 3 | B | Answer choice B is correct. Stair is the correct spelling as the word is used in the sentence. Option A is a homophone. Option C is another word for guiding. |
| 4 | B | Threw is the correct word to use in the above sentence. The others are homophones. |
| 5 | B | The first word is an adverb meaning "very," and the second word is an adjective meaning "not loud." |
| 6 | A | Answer choice A has the correct spelling of the word. Options C and D make sense but are not spelled correctly. |
| 7 | C | Answer choice C has the correct spelling of the word. |
| 8 | A | Answer choice A has the correct spelling of the word. |
| 9 | C | Answer choice C has the correct spelling of the word. |
| 10 | D | Answer choice D has the correct spelling of principal as it is used in the sentence. Option A is spelled correctly, but the definition does not make sense in the sentence. |
| 11 | telescope | Telescope is the instrument with which we can see far away objects in the sky |
| 12 | itinerary | It is a planned route or journey. |

# Lesson 10: Vary Sentences

| Question No. | Answer | Detailed Explanations |
|---|---|---|
| 1 | D | The sentences can be combined to make a compound sentence using the conjunction so. The correct answer is D. |
| 2 | A | The sentences can be combined to make a compound sentence using the conjunction but. The correct answer is A. |
| 3 | C | The sentences can best be combined by listing the different things that will be at the party using commas to separate items in a series. |
| 4 | A | The sentence fragment, after school, can be used as a dependent clause to make a complex sentence. The correct answer is A. |
| 5 | D | To keep the sentences from being repetitive, they can be combined together. Answer choice D makes the most sense. |
| 6 | C | Since the author likes both summer and spring but spring best, it is best to combine these sentences into a compound sentence using the contrasting conjunction but. |
| 7 | B | The sentence fragment can be turned into a dependent clause to create a complex sentence. The correct answer is B. |
| 8 | C | Since the author is listing things they have to do, combining each task and separating them with commas is the best way to combine these sentences. The correct answer is C. |
| 9 | A | Combining the two sentences into one simple sentence is the best option. The correct answer is A. |
| 10 | B | Using the adjective brown to describe the puppy and listing its other attributes creates the best sentence. The correct answer is B. |

# Lesson 11: Maintain Consistency in Style and Tone

| Question No. | Answer | Detailed Explanations |
|---|---|---|
| 1 | A | While each sentence says basically the same thing, only the first sentence paints the clearest picture of what was actually happening.  The correct answer is A. |
| 2 | B | While each sentence has the same meaning, sentence B uses the most descriptive words and style. |
| 3 | D | Each sentence adds just a little more detail to better explain the topic.  Answer choice D is correct. |
| 4 | B | Answer choice A appears to be too choppy while answer choice C is too short.  The best answer choice is B. |
| 5 | D | Sometimes fewer words, and more to the point is best.  The correct answer choice is D. |
| 6 | C | Even though there are still 2 sentences, answer choice C maintains the best style and tone for the sentences. |
| 7 | A | Choices A and D are both possible; however, answer choice A offers a more varied and imaginative sentence style. |
| 8 | B | Answer choice B has the best overall style and tone of the four choices. |
| 9 | B | While Beth thought the test was challenging, Mary thought it was easy. |
| 10 | C | Answer choice C uses the smoothest language while creating a picture of what is going on. |

# Lesson 12: Use Clues to Determine Multiple-Meaning Words

| Question No. | Answer | Detailed Explanations |
|---|---|---|
| 1 | C | According to the passage, crabs and shrimp are crustaceans. That is specifically said in the passage. |
| 2 | A | An exoskeleton is a skeleton outside the body, so the answer is A. |
| 3 | B | Bio means life, so a biopolymer is a stubstance is found in living things. |
| 4 | A | This is a figurative expression and is not to be taken literally. Answer choice A is correct. It means they have more projects coming. |
| 5 | B | Smelly has a negative connotation; fragrant is positive. Based on what the paragraph says, these smell good. |
| 6 | B | Attracted and accepted do not mean the same thing as housed. Held means that they were in that branch, so that's the same meaning as housed. |
| 7 | C | The definition of brake that is used in this sentence is answer choice C. |
| 8 | B | Alive and dead are the only opposites listed in the above answer choices, so the correct answer is B. |
| 9 | D | If the volume of traffic was high, that means there was a lot of traffic on the interstate. The correct answer is D. |
| 10 | C | If you are earning something, that means it is an extra amount, so the answer is C. |
| 11 | B | All of the other answer choices are synonyms. The only pair of opposites is answer choice B. |
| 12 | A | The only pair of opposite words is answer choice A. |
| 13 | C | The only answer choice containing a pair of opposite words is answer choice C. |

# Lesson 13: Use Context Clues to Determine Word Meaning

| Question No. | Answer | Detailed Explanations |
|---|---|---|
| 1 | B | Julio was happy, not disappointed, but the text tells us that he wa also something else. Satisfied and pleased are very similar to happy so they are not something else. He expected other boys to win th title, so the best use of context to figure out the word "astounded" is to select "very surprised." |
| 2 | C | The signal word "but" tells us that the opposite of flimsy is strong because spider silk is stronger than steel. |
| 3 | A | The text tells us what is on every side of New Jersey, so we know that bordered is the same thing as surrounded by. |
| 4 | A | Answer A is the answer that makes the most sense. Africa is large so none of the other answers make sense. |
| 5 | A | Never leaving someone means that you are loyal. Answer choice A is correct. |
| 6 | C | Based on the sentence, beneficial means good for you. Doctor wouldn't tell you to do it unless it was good for you. |
| 7 | D | Because it was unbearable, we know that the smell was awful. The correct answer is D. |
| 8 | A | Because the celebrity was overwhelmed, we know there were a lo of questions. For that reason, the answer is A. |
| 9 | C | Because it was summer, we know that sweltering means hot. I would never be cold on a beach in the summer. |
| 10 | Ugly | We know that it will be a word with a negative connotation and the only negative word that fits the sentence . |
| 11 | hesitant | The sentence specifically says that he was afraid of scary movies. |
| 12 | Wet | Because it had been out in the rain, we can assume that it was soak ing wet and not just damp. |

# Lesson 14: Use Common Roots and Affixes

| Question No. | Answer | Detailed Explanations |
|---|---|---|
| 1 | D | An affix can either be a prefix or a suffix, but a suffix will never be at the beginning of a word. Suffixes are only at the ends of words. The correct answer is D. |
| 2 | A | Incapable and not being able to do something are the same thing, so the only possible answer is A. |
| 3 | C | "-age" is the suffix that is the same in all three words. The correct answer is C. |
| 4 | B | "An-" is the only prefix that all three words have in common. The correct answer is B. |
| 5 | C | "Less" means "without," so the answer is C. |
| 6 | A | "-Ology" is the study of, so the answer is A. Although option D mentions study, -ology is not only the study of animals. |
| 7 | Comm | "Comm-" means "together,". |
| 8 | C | Both A and B are true, so the answer is C. |
| 9 | B | This is a two syllable word, so there should only be one hyphen between the n and the t. The answer is B. |
| 10 | D | Monarch only has two syllables, so it will only have one hyphen when you divide it. The hyphen should be between the two syllables, which is the case in answer choice D. |
| 11 | dia | The prefix that the three words have in common is dia. |
| 12 | yield | yield or surrender is the exact definition of cede. |

# Lesson 15: Consult Reference Materials

| Question No. | Answer | Detailed Explanations |
|---|---|---|
| 1 | B | Alphabetize means to rearrange the words in the order that they would appear in the dictionary. Answer choice B is the only one where the words are correctly alphabetized. |
| 2 | D | Alphabetize means to rearrange the words in the order that they would appear in the dictionary. Answer choice D is the only one where the words are alphabetized correctly. |
| 3 | D | Alphabetize means to rearrange the words in the order that they would appear in the dictionary. Answer choice D is the only one where the words are alphabetized correctly. |
| 4 | D | The dictionary contains all of these things, so answer choice D is true. |
| 5 | C | A synonym is what you find in the thesaurus. That is where you go when you're looking for a new word to replace an existing word. |
| 6 | B | Dictionaries are in alphabetical order, so answer choice B is correct. |
| 7 | D | Guidewords are at the top and guide you in your search for the word. They allow you to figure out if the word you are looking up falls within the guidewords for that page. |
| 8 | | Organized is 3 syllables. |
| 9 | C | Jacket is 2 syllables, so the answer is C. |
| 10 | B | It has 3 syllables, so answer choice B is correct. |
| 11 | | objective, obligation, obscure, obsess are the words alphabetized correctly. |
| 12 | | hence, hero, hesitate, hibernate are the words alphabetized correctly. |

# Lesson 16: Determine the Meaning of a Word

| Question No. | Answer | Detailed Explanations |
|---|---|---|
| 1 | B | Based upon the usage in the sentence, the word "misplaced" means to lose. The correct answer is B. |
| 2 | C | While the word "brisk" can mean both fast and cool, in this particular sentence it means "cool." The correct answer is C. |
| 3 | C | Since Natalie and Sophia are looking forward to their ride, the answer must have a positive connotation. The correct answer is "exciting," C. |
| 4 | D | Mundane means repetitive or boring. The correct answer choice is D. The context clues in the sentences help you determine this. |
| 5 | A | "Ravenous" means to be hungry. The correct answer is A. The context clues in the sentences help you determine this. |
| 6 | D | To triumph over someone or something means to win. The correct answer is D. |
| 7 | B | For something to be "bewitching" then it has captured your attention in a positive way. The correct answer is "charming," B. |
| 8 | D | Julia does not enjoy fishing, therefore it must be awful. The correct answer is D. The context clues in the sentences help you determine this. |
| 9 | A | In the context of the sentence, "perspective" means look or appearance. The correct answer is A. |
| 10 | D | A dictionary, thesaurus, and glossary can all give you an idea of what a word means. The correct answer is D, "All of the above." |

# Lesson 17: Interpret Figures of Speech

| Question No. | Answer | Detailed Explanations |
|---|---|---|
| 1 | D | The sentence uses the repeated sound /j/ so it is an example of alliteration and a comparison using "like" so it is also an example of a simile. |
| 2 | A | The sentence does not mean to literally not spill the beans but rather not tell a secret. The correct answer is A, idiom. |
| 3 | B | The sentence is comparing a sandwich to a car using "as" which means it is a simile. |
| 4 | A | An extreme exaggeration is an example of hyperbole. |
| 5 | C | The sentence is giving human like characteristics to a bear. This is personification. |
| 6 | D | A word that represents its sound is onomatopoeia. |
| 7 | B | The sentence is comparing Katy to a pig without using "like" or "as." This is a metaphor. |
| 8 | B | An extreme exaggeration is an example of hyperbole. |
| 9 | Idiom | "Stop pulling my leg" does not mean that someone is literally pulling one's leg. It means to stop teasing. This is an idiom. |
| 10 | Simile | The sentence compares Danielle's dancing to a swan using "as." It is a simile. |
| 11 | | Simile is a figure of speech that directly compares two things using words such as like, as, so, than, etc

Metaphor is a figure of speech in which an implied comparison is made between two unlike things that actually have something in common

Personification is a figure of speech in which an implied comparison is made between two unlike things that actually have something in common

Hence, He is as cunning as a fox - is a simile

The world is a stage is a metaphor and

The fire swallowed the entire forest is personification. |

# Lesson 18: Use Relationships to Better Understand Words

| Question No. | Answer | Detailed Explanations |
| --- | --- | --- |
| 1 | A | The reason the flights were cancelled was the blizzard, so answer choice A is the only one that is correct. |
| 2 | B | The flood is what caused the people to be left homeless, so answer choice B is correct. |
| 3 | C | Pedro got the job because of his friendly attitude, so answer choice C is correct. |
| 4 | A | Answer choice A is correct because the only mammal listed is giraffe. |
| 5 | A | The only bird listed is a parrot, so A is correct. |
| 6 | B | The only dessert listed is pie, so B is the correct answer. |
| 7 | C | Answer choice C is the only one that puts things in the correct order. |
| 8 | B | Bees are the only insect listed, so answer choice B is correct. |
| 9 | B | The smoky smell was caused by the burned popcorn, so answer choice B is correct. |
| 10 | C | Answer choice C is the only one that shows the correct cause and effect. |
| 11 |  | Cause - daylight savings time. Effect - The evenings are longer. The evenings are longer because of daylight savings time. |
| 12 |  | Cause - Whistling at work;  Effect - Task becomes easier |
| 13 |  | Cause - The street sweeper. Effect - The noise. The noise is caused by the street sweeper. |

# Lesson 19: Distinguish Between Word Associations and Definitions

| Question No. | Answer | Detailed Explanations |
|:---:|:---:|:---|
| 1 | B | "Denotation" is the dictionary or literal meaning of a word. The correct answer is B. |
| 2 | C | "Connotation" refers to how the word makes us feel. The correct answer is C. |
| 3 | D | All the words listed have the same denotation as the word "house." |
| 4 | C | A child is often referred to as an adolescent. The correct answer is C. |
| 5 | C | Answer choices A and B, are structurally similar but the words have no similarities other than that. Answer choice D is opposites. Answer choice C is the correct answer. |
| 6 | D | Answer choice A and B are both antonyms so they do not have the same denotation. Horse and rabbits are similar in that they are both mammals but they do not have the same denotation. The correct answer is D. |
| 7 | D | The word "cheap" has a negative connotation to it. |
| 8 | B | The word Flop is not quite as hard as disaster therefore it has a positive connotation. |
| 9 | A | When thinking about something being messy, "filthy" is the answer choice that is the most negative. |
| 10 | C | A nice, or positive, way to say old is to say that someone is "elderly." |

# Lesson 20: Use Grade Appropriate Words

| Question No. | Answer | Detailed Explanations |
|---|---|---|
| 1 | B | Answer choice B is an example of the word racket when it means noise. |
| 2 | D | In answer choice D, since the person has to bear weight or hold themselves up on their broken ankle, it is the correct answer. |
| 3 | C | If the little boy is being patient in line then he is quietly waiting. The correct answer is C. |
| 4 | B | Pounding on something until it breaks would be pounding to hit. The correct answer is B. |
| 5 | A | A pack or group of wolves mean that answer choice A is correct. |
| 6 | B | Since the author uses the words "even though they studied" it gives the impression that they did not feel too confident about their test. This would mean they felt anxious. The correct answer choice is B. |
| 7 | A | While the Grand Canyon is brown and stationary it is not small. The best word to describe it would be immense. The correct answer is A. |
| 8 | D | If a person needs to spend extra time training for a race then it probably is not easy or smooth. The correct answer choice is D, rigorous. |
| 9 | A | If Joey got caught cheating then he probably got himself into a predicament. The correct answer is A. |
| 10 | D | The best thing a team could be would be diligent about practicing. The correct answer choice is D. |

## OST FAQs

### What will OST Assessment Look Like?

In many ways, the OST assessments will be unlike anything many students have ever seen. The tests will be conducted online, requiring students complete tasks to assess a deeper understanding of the Ohio Learning standards. The students will take the Summative Assessment at the end of the year. The time for the ELA Summative assessment for each grade is given below:

| Estimated Time on Task in Minutes | | |
|---|---|---|
| Grade | Part 1 | Part 2 |
| 3 | 90 | 90 |
| 4 | 90 | 90 |
| 5 | 90 | 90 |
| 6 | 105 | 105 |
| 7 | 105 | 105 |
| 8 | 105 | 105 |

### How is this Lumos tedBook aligned to OST Guidelines?

The practice tests provided in the Lumos Program were created to reflect the depth and rigor of the OST assessments based on the information published by the test administrator. However, the content and format of the OST assessment that is officially administered to the students could be different compared to these practice tests. You can get more information about this test by visiting The ohio department of education website.

### What item types are included in the Online OST Test?

Because the assessment is online, the test will consist of a combination of new types of questions:

1. Drag and Drop
2. Evidence based selected response (EBSR)
3. Extended Constructed Response
4. Hot Text Selective Highlight
5. Drop Down
6. Multiple Choice – Single Correct Response, radial buttons
7. Table Fill-in
8. Multiple Choice – Multiple Response, check boxes
9. Matching Table
10. Numeric Response
11. Grid

Spring Assessment for 2019-20 has been canceled.
For more information on 2020-21 Assessment year, Visit
**http://www.lumoslearning.com/a/ost-2021-faqs**
OR Scan the **QR Code**

## How Can the Lumos Study Program Prepare Students for OST Tests?

At Lumos Learning, we believe that year-long learning and adequate practice before the actual test are the keys to success on OST test. We have designed the Lumos study program to help students get plenty of realistic practice before the test and to promote year-long collaborative learning.

This is a Lumos tedBook™. It connects you to Online OST Assessments and additional resources. You can access these resources using a number of devices including personal computers, Android/iOS phones and tablets. The Lumos StepUp Online Assessment is designed to promote year-long learning. It is a simple program students can securely access using a computer or device with internet access. Students will get instant feedback and can review their answers anytime. Each student's answers and progress can be reviewed by parents and educators to reinforce the learning experience.

## Why Practice with Repeated Reading Passages?

Throughout the Lumos Learning Practice workbooks, students and educators will notice many passages repeat. This is done intentionally. The goal of these workbooks is to help students practice skills necessary to be successful in class and on standardized tests. One of the most critical components to that success is the ability to read and comprehend passages. To that end, reading fluency must be strengthened. According to Hasbrouck and Tindal (2006), "Helping our students become fluent readers is absolutely critical for proficient and motivated reading" (p. 642). And, Nichols et al. indicate, (2009), "fluency is a gateway to comprehension that enables students to move from being word decoders to passage comprehenders" (p. 11).

Lumos Learning recognizes there is no one-size-fits-all approach to build fluency in readers; however, the repeated reading of passages, where students read the same passages at least two or more times, is one of the most widely recognized strategies to improve fluency (Nichols et al., 2009). Repeated reading allows students the opportunity to read passages with familiar words several times until the passage becomes familiar and they no longer have to decode word by word. As students reread, the decoding barrier falls away allowing for an increase in reading comprehension.

The goal of the Lumos Learning workbooks is to increase student achievement and preparation for any standardized test. Using some passages multiple times in a book offers struggling readers an opportunity to do just that.

References
Hasbrouck, J., and Tindal, G. (2006). Oral reading fluency norms: A valuable assessment tool for reading teachers. Reading Teacher, 59(7), 636644. doi:10.1598/RT.59.7.3.
Nichols, W., Rupley, W., and Rasinski, T. (2009). Fluency in learning to read for meaning: going beyond repeated readings. Literacy Research & Instruction, 48(1). doi:10.1080/19388070802161906.

# Discover Engaging and Relevant Learning Resources

Lumos EdSearch is a safe search engine specifically designed for teachers and students. Using EdSearch, you can easily find thousands of standards-aligned learning resources such as questions, videos, lessons, worksheets and apps. Teachers can use EdSearch to create custom resource kits to perfectly match their lesson objective and assign them to one or more students in their classroom.

To access the EdSearch tool, use the search box after you log into Lumos StepUp or use the link provided below.

| | |
|---|---|
| http://www.lumoslearning.com/a/edsearchb |  |

**The Lumos Standards Coherence map** provides information about previous level, next level and related standards. It helps educators and students visually explore learning standards. It's an effective tool to help students progress through the learning objectives. Teachers can use this tool to develop their own pacing charts and lesson plans. Educators can also use the coherence map to get deep insights into why a student is struggling in a specific learning objective.

Teachers can access the Coherence maps after logging into the StepUp Teacher Portal or use the link provided below.

| | |
|---|---|
| http://www.lumoslearning.com/a/coherence-map |  |

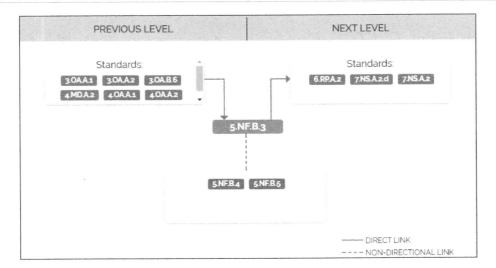

# What if I buy more than one Lumos Study Program?

**Step 1**

**Visit the URL and login to your account.**
http://www.lumoslearning.com

**Step 2**

Click on 'My tedBooks' under the "Account" tab.
Place the Book Access Code and submit.

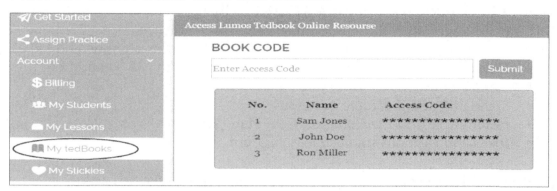

**Step 3**

To add the new book for a registered student, choose the ○ Existing Student button and select the student and submit.

To add the new book for a new student, choose the ● Add New student button and complete the student registration.

Assign To ⊙

○ Existing Student          ● Add New student

Register Your TedBook

Student Name:*          Enter First Name          Enter Last Name

Student Login*

Password*

Submit

# Lumos StepUp® Mobile App FAQ For Students

## What is the Lumos StepUp® App?

It is a FREE application you can download onto your Android Smartphones, tablets, iPhones, and iPads.

## What are the Benefits of the StepUp® App?

This mobile application gives convenient access to Practice Tests, Common Core State Standard Online Workbooks, and learning resources through your Smartphone and tablet computers.

- Eleven Technology enhanced question types in both MATH and ELA
- Sample questions for Arithmetic drills
- Standard specific sample questions
- Instant access to the Common Core State Standards
- Jokes and cartoons to make learning fun!

## Do I Need the StepUp® App to Access Online Workbooks?

No, you can access Lumos StepUp® Online Workbooks through a personal computer. The StepUp app simply enhances your learning experience and allows you to conveniently access StepUp Online Workbooks and additional resources through your smartphone or tablet.

## How can I Download the App?

Visit **lumoslearning.com/a/stepup-app** using your Smartphone or tablet and follow the instruction to download the app.

**QR Code
for Smartphone
Or Tablet Users**

# Lumos StepUp® Mobile App FAQ
# For Parents and Teachers

## What is the Lumos StepUp® App?

It is a free app that teachers can use to easily access real-time student activity information as well as assign learning resources to students. Parents can also use it to easily access school-related information such as homework assigned by teachers and PTA meetings. It can be downloaded onto smartphones and tablets from popular App Stores.

## What are the Benefits of the Lumos StepUp® App?

It provides convenient access to

- Standards aligned learning resources for your students
- An easy to use Dashboard
- Student progress reports
- Active and inactive students in your classroom
- Professional development information
- Educational Blogs

## How can I Download the App?

Visit **lumoslearning.com/a/stepup-app** using your Smartphone or tablet and follow the instructions to download the app.

**QR Code
for Smartphone
Or Tablet Users**

# Progress Chart

| Standard | Lesson | Page No. | Practice | | Mastered | Re-practice /Reteach |
|---|---|---|---|---|---|---|
| CCSS | | | Date | Score | | |
| RL.6.1 | Analysis of Key Events and Ideas | 11 | | | | |
| RL.6.1 | Conclusions Drawn from the Text | 21 | | | | |
| RL.6.2 | Development of Ideas | 29 | | | | |
| RL.6.2 | Summary of Text | 38 | | | | |
| RL.6.3 | Characters Responses and Changes | 45 | | | | |
| RL.6.4 | Figurative Words and Phrases | 55 | | | | |
| RL.6.4 | Connotative Words and Phrases | 60 | | | | |
| RL.6.4 | Meaning of Words and Phrases | 64 | | | | |
| RL.6.5 | Develop Setting | 69 | | | | |
| RL.6.6 | Author's Purpose in a Text | 79 | | | | |
| RL.6.9 | Compare Author's Writing to Another | 83 | | | | |
| RI.6.1 | Cite Textual Evidence | 105 | | | | |
| RI.6.2 | Central Idea of Text | 111 | | | | |
| RI.6.3 | Analyze How People, Events, or Ideas are Presented in Text | 117 | | | | |
| RI.6.4 | Determine Technical Meanings | 124 | | | | |
| RI.6.5 | Structure of Text | 129 | | | | |
| RI.6.6 | Determine Author's Point of View | 135 | | | | |
| RI.6.8 | Evaluating Arguments in Text | 141 | | | | |
| RI.6.9 | Compare/Contrast One Author's Presentation with Another | 148 | | | | |

| Standard | Lesson | Page No. | Practice | | Mastered | Re-practice /Reteach |
|---|---|---|---|---|---|---|
| CCSS | | | Date | Score | | |
| ..6.1 | Correct subject-verb agreement | 166 | | | | |
| ..6.1.A | Correct Use of Adjectives and Adverbs | 170 | | | | |
| ..6.1.B | Recognize Pronouns | 174 | | | | |
| ..6.1.C | Recognize and Correct Shifts in Pronoun | 178 | | | | |
| ..6.1.D | Recognize and Correct Vague Pronouns | 181 | | | | |
| ..6.1.E | Recognize Variations in English | 184 | | | | |
| ..6.2 | Demonstrate command of Capitalization | 187 | | | | |
| ..6.2.A | Demonstrate Command of Punctuation | 191 | | | | |
| ..6.2.B | Correct Spelling | 195 | | | | |
| ..6.3.A | Vary Sentences | 199 | | | | |
| ..6.3.B | Maintain Consistency in Style and Tone | 203 | | | | |
| ..6.4 | Use Clues To Determine Multiple-meaning Words | 206 | | | | |
| ..6.4.A | Use Context Clues to Determine Word Meaning | 211 | | | | |
| ..6.4.B | Use Common Roots and Affixes | 215 | | | | |
| ..6.4.C | Consult Reference Materials | 219 | | | | |
| ..6.4.D | Determine the Meaning of a Word | 223 | | | | |
| ..6.5.A | Interpret Figures of Speech | 226 | | | | |
| ..6.5.B | Use Relationships to Better Understand Words | 230 | | | | |
| ..6.5.C | Distinguish Between Word Associations and Definitions | 234 | | | | |
| ..6.6 | Use Grade Appropriate Words | 237 | | | | |

**Lumos Learning**
Developed by Expert Teachers

# Grade 6

# OHIO
# Math
## OST Practice

## UPDATED for 2020-21

ONLINE

**2 OST Practice Tests**

**11 Question Types**

## COVERS 30+ SKILLS

Ohio Department of Education does not sponsor or endorse this product.

# Available

- At Leading book stores
- Online www.LumosLearning.com

Made in the USA
Coppell, TX
31 March 2021